WHY IS THE WORLD SO BEAUTIFUL?

Also by Nicholas Humphrey

Consciousness Regained: Chapters in the Development of Mind

In a Dark Time (edited with Robert Jay Lifton)

The Inner Eye: Social Intelligence in Evolution

A History of the Mind: Evolution and the Birth of Consciousness

Leaps of Faith: Science, Miracles, and the Search for Supernatural Consolation

How to Solve the Mind-Body Problem

The Mind Made Flesh: Essays from the Frontiers of Evolution and Psychology

Seeing Red: A Study in Consciousness

Soul Dust: The Magic of Consciousness

Sentience: The Invention of Consciousness

WHY IS THE WORLD SO BEAUTIFUL?

OUR MINDS IN SEARCH OF NATURE'S RHYMES

NICHOLAS HUMPHREY

The MIT Press
Cambridge, Massachusetts
London, England

The MIT Press
Massachusetts Institute of Technology
77 Massachusetts Avenue, Cambridge, MA 02139
mitpress.mit.edu

The MIT Press would like to thank the anonymous peer reviewers who provided comments on drafts of this book. The generous work of academic experts is essential for establishing the authority and quality of our publications. We acknowledge with gratitude the contributions of these otherwise uncredited readers.

This book was set in ITC Stone Serif Std and ITC Stone Sans Std by New Best-set Typesetters Ltd. Printed and bound in the United States of America.

Library of Congress Cataloging-in-Publication Data

Names: Humphrey, Nicholas author
Title: Why is the world so beautiful? : our minds in search of nature's rhymes / Nicholas Humphrey.
Description: Cambridge, Massachusetts : The MIT Press, [2026] | Includes bibliographical references and index.
Identifiers: LCCN 2026002021 (print) | LCCN 2026002022 (ebook) | ISBN 9780262056588 hardcover | ISBN 9780262056595 pdf | ISBN 9780262056601 epub
Subjects: LCSH: Aesthetics—Psychological aspects | Neuropsychology | Evolution (Biology)
Classification: LCC BH301.P78 H86 2026 (print) | LCC BH301.P78 (ebook)
LC record available at https://lccn.loc.gov/2026002021
LC ebook record available at https://lccn.loc.gov/2026002022

10 9 8 7 6 5 4 3 2 1

EU authorized representative: Easy Access System Europe, Mustamäe tee 50, 10621 Tallinn, Estonia | Email: gpsr.requests@easproject.com

In memory of
Gerard Manley Hopkins, poet (1844–1889)
Daniel Dennett, philosopher (1942–2024)
Two superb rhymers

The MIT Press's publishing mission benefits from the generosity of our donors, including Hyun-A Park and Jacob Friis.

CONTENTS

PREFACE

For many years I've wanted to read a book called *Why Is the World So Beautiful?* Not finding it in any library, I've now written it myself. Whether this is the book I wanted to read I'm not yet sure. I think it could be. But I confess the writing has taken its own path and I've surprised myself along the way.

I don't suppose you will find it to be the book you are expecting either. Some readers may be disappointed that I have little to say about modern neuroscience (it's because, as you'll see, I think neuroscience has little to say about beauty). Some may be taken aback by the way I've introduced "God, the artist," into a book about human psychology (it's because I think aesthetic emotion is intimately linked to the idea of a creator.) Some may wonder why I haven't made a connection to my earlier writings about phenomenal consciousness (it's because I raise new issues here; and, in any case, I've read the consciousness book already and found it incomplete).

I know that expectations unfulfilled can be a problem. My young daughter regularly ended her birthday in tears, not because she didn't like her gifts but because she imagined something different. In a famous experiment, from 1920, it was shown that when a monkey expected to find a piece of banana under a cup and found instead a piece of lettuce, he threw a tantrum and refused to eat the lettuce.

I hope you'll find as you read on that in developing a science of beauty, old-fashioned God-linked lettuce has a lot to recommend it (and more than its imaginary rivals).

The book is dedicated to the philosopher Daniel Dennett, whose love of rhyme in art and science went as deep as anyone's and to the poet Gerard Manley Hopkins whose love of God made him akin to Dan.

When I first made forays into evolutionary aesthetics in the 1970s, I was lucky to have the backing of two mentors, the psychologist Richard Gregory and the art historian Ernst Gombrich. Fifty years later, I'm glad to have had critical readings of the book from their successors Geoffrey Lloyd, Martin Rees, Paul Broks, Chris McManus, Philip Steadman, and Keith Frankish. In bringing it to press, Philip Laughlin, my editor at MIT, and Toby Mundy, my literary agent, have provided unfailing encouragement.

1 "THE ARGUMENT FROM BEAUTY"

Some years ago, I was involved in making a documentary film about a family of human hand-walkers. Five children, with a genetic mutation that affected the brain's cerebellum, never learned to stand upright and continued as adults to walk on all fours (figure 1.1).

FIGURE 1.1
Children of the Ulas family. Iskenderun, Turkey, 2005. Photo by Jon Lane. © Passionate Productions 2006. By kind permission of Jemima Harrison.

They lived in a small village in southern Turkey, about thirty kilometers from the coast. But their lives were so constrained that they had not ever visited the sea. We arranged to take them on an outing to a deserted beach. The children—now in their twenties and thirties—were excited beyond measure. They raced down to the water's edge where the waves were breaking. The mother and father sat at the top of the beach, gazing in wonderment. "I never knew," exclaimed the mother, "Allah had created such a beautiful world."[1]

In several respects, the world this family inhabited was far from beautiful. The children's mental and physical abnormalities meant that life was a constant struggle. They were poor. They were spurned and mistreated by other villagers. Yet the local imam had explained to the parents that all was as God intended. These children were given as a test of the parents' ability to cope with adversity (for which they would be rewarded in the afterlife).

Remarkably, no one was complaining. The parents had succeeded astonishingly well in raising and sheltering their offspring. The children themselves seemed not to be unhappy. They smiled and joked and fooled around with their siblings. They took pleasure in cooking and doing needlework and odd jobs. They enjoyed occasional trips by van to the local hospital for medical checkups. When we provided them with walking frames, they eagerly rose to the challenge and laughed at their own clumsiness. Without question, they loved each other. And the parents, far from resenting their lot, went along with the imam's interpretation and thanked God for their blessings. Indeed, they remained open to new signs of his beneficence.

When the mother, sitting on the beach, saw with her own eyes the beauty of the scene in front of her—the sun sparkling on the sea, the rolling waves, the fruit of her womb gamboling across the strand—her mind turned immediately to the creator. Art implies an artist. Praise be to Allah.

* * *

We have here the main elements of the puzzle I address in this book. Or, as it may be, a nest of puzzles. *Why is the world so beautiful?*

People recognize beauty on many levels and in many contexts—beautiful faces, beautiful flowers, beautiful sunsets, beautiful music, beautiful deeds, beautiful ideas. Philosophers have sometimes tried to mark off "true beauty" as a rarefied quality to which only the most discerning human beings respond. But I'm concerned here with kinds of beauty that touch everybody's lives. So I spread the net broadly to include things we might otherwise call delightful or enchanting or lovely. In every case, what's at issue is a quality that goes beyond the power to please our bodily senses.

Beauty delights the mind. To qualify, a thing must possess a combination of properties that—by virtue of internal harmonies, rhymes, balance, relationships without or within—make of the parts a beautiful whole. Thus, a wildflower meadow can be beautiful but not a field of grass. An air on a G string but not a single note. An argument but not a statement of fact.

When the combination *works* for us in a particular way, we experience a unique "aesthetic emotion." The thing strikes us as being just right. It seems we have arrived. The result is that we may experience a kind of stillness. But it's an energized stillness. The poet Samuel Taylor Coleridge put it well: "Sometimes when I earnestly look at a beautiful object or landscape, it seems as if I were on the *brink* of a fruition still denied—as if Vision were an *appetite*; even as a man would feel, who having put forth all his muscular strength in an act of prosilience, is at the very moment *held back*—he leaps and yet moves not from his place."[2]

We feel joy that such a thing exists, but we don't stop there. We no sooner encounter beauty of this kind than we feel the *want* of it, the urge to secure it. As Jorge Luis Borges described it: "Music, states of happiness, mythology, faces belabored by time, certain twilights and certain places try to tell us something, or have said something we should not have missed, or are about to say something; this imminence of a revelation which does not occur is, perhaps, the aesthetic phenomenon."[3] So beauty can make us vulnerable. It creates a void and—temporarily—fills it.

We wonder at beauty. Wonder at it and wonder about it. But the greatest wonder of all could be that there's so much of it about. Perhaps more than we should reasonably expect—perhaps more than we humans require or deserve. Why is there so much of *this* in the world? Why are we so lucky?

I'll make the question more specific: How can we explain the remarkable convergence between what human beings find beautiful and what the world at large has on display?

* * *

One answer is that of the mother on the Turkish beach: It's Allah. And that answer is not just hers. Many people assume that the fact that the world is so beautiful does indeed cry out for explanation. It cannot be accidental. Effects must have causes. And, for the religiously minded, the first cause that comes to mind is God. They are supported by theologians who, arguing the other way round—from the effect to the cause—consider "the argument from beauty" to be one of the best reasons to believe in God's existence to begin with.

The argument from beauty follows the same logic as the better-known argument from design as set out by William Paley in his 1802 treatise, *Natural Theology: or, Evidences of the Existence and Attributes of the Deity Collected from the Appearances of Nature*. Suppose, said Paley, we were to stumble across an ingenious pocket watch lying in the grass. We'd be right to assume that a skilled human being must have had a hand in its design. So, likewise, when we find in nature a brilliantly constructed biological mechanism such as the human eye, we can assume that an intelligent deity must have designed it. Extending this argument to beauty, if we were to come across an artwork such as the *Mona Lisa* on the walls of a cave, we could assume that a human artist must be responsible. And when we find things of comparable beauty in nature—the song of a nightingale, say, or the aurora borealis—we can only conclude that a divine artist has created them.

To complete the argument, we can usefully add a further premise. The Bible's book of Genesis tells us that God himself was pleased with his seven-day creation. Day by day, "he saw that it was good" And on the sixth day, when he created human beings, he created beings capable of seeing just how good it was. For he made a point of instilling in humans an *aesthetic sense*—the capacity to admire the craftsmanship and beauty of the world around them, so that they would look up to him and love him. In the words of the hymn:[4]

All things bright and beautiful,
All creatures great and small,
All things wise and wonderful,
The Lord God made them all.

He gave us eyes to see them,
And lips that we might tell

How great is God Almighty,
Who has made all things well.

* * *

On the face of it, these arguments may seem attractive and even reasonable. However, their attraction depends on there being no *more* reasonable explanation of the facts. And this has made both arguments vulnerable to progress in the natural sciences.

Most scientists now agree that the argument from design was blown away in the nineteenth century by Charles Darwin's theory of evolution. Darwin showed how the blind process of natural selection could do the work of the intelligent designer to create near-perfect feats of biological engineering. Can it be shown that natural selection (or any other known natural process) could do the work of the divine artist to create a world with so much beauty on display?

Modern advocates of the argument from beauty are certainly sensitive to the possibility of naturalistic explanations.[5] But they have been quick to point out that any *utilitarian explanation,* such as natural selection, can go only so far. It may be able to explain why the love of beautiful objects would have spread among our ancestors if and when those who are attracted to such objects were more likely to survive and pass on their genes. And it might explain why objects that display beauty would have spread if and when the qualities that make them attractive ensure they are more likely to be copied and preserved. But how can it explain the existence of "useless beauty"—where neither of these forces is at work?

The point is well taken. Humans' love of beauty undoubtedly extends to objects that have no obvious bearing on human survival. Think of the scrolled head of a fern, the song of a blackbird, mountains reflected in a lake. In fact, the lack of utility may go further still. Not only is the beautiful object of no use to us, but its beauty of no use to *the object itself.* Being beautiful is doing nothing to sustain it or keep it in the picture. Think of a pearl, a rainbow, the starry sky.

For some philosophers, uselessness has been taken to be a key element of beauty. The philosopher Immanuel Kant opined: "When the question is whether a thing be beautiful, we do not want to know whether anything depends or can depend, for us or for anyone else, on the existence of the object, but only how we estimate it in pure contemplation."[6] The poet Theophile Gautier was still more adamant: "There is nothing really beautiful except that which can be of no use."[7]

But if *we* don't benefit from interacting with objects we find beautiful and *the objects* don't benefit from having features that appear beautiful to us, what can be keeping all this beauty going? *Cui bono?*

* * *

I admit that science is short of answers here. We could simply declare a truce (render unto science the things that are science's but unto God the things that are God's). But I'm writing this book to try to recover the scientific initiative. And, notwithstanding the skeptics, I'm going to prioritize evolutionary explanations.

Two hundred fifty years ago, the remarkable Scottish philosopher Thomas Reid suggested the way forward: "All the objects we call beautiful agree in two things, which seem to concur in our sense of beauty. First, when they are perceived, or even imagined, they produce a certain agreeable emotion or feeling in the mind; and secondly, this agreeable emotion is accompanied with an opinion or belief of their having some perfection or excellence belonging to them."[8]

The belief, Reid notes, is *instinctive*: "Objects strike us at once, and appear beautiful at first sight, without any reflection, without our being able to say why we call them beautiful or being able to specify any perfection which justifies our judgment. The beauty of the object may, in such cases, be called an occult quality. We know well how it affects our senses; but what it is in itself we know not."[9]

Nonetheless, says Reid, if we were to look further, it ought to be possible to discover why in most cases our judgment is justified: "By a careful examination of the objects to which Nature hath given this amiable quality [of Beauty], we may perhaps discover some real excellence in the object, or, at least, some valuable purpose that is served by the effect which it produces upon us. This instinctive sense of beauty, in different species of animals, may differ as much as the external sense of taste, and in each species be adapted to its manner of life."[10]

Reid was a probing philosopher, and he recognized that we still have to explain just *why* there should be a connection between perceiving a thing's excellence and feeling the agreeable emotion. But he was writing one hundred years before Darwin, and he did not have a scientific theory of biological adaptation to fall back on. Perhaps, he suggested rather weakly, the connection is logically necessary (so it would be self-contradictory to say, for example, "I see the excellence of a rainbow but don't feel the beauty"). Or perhaps—but he does not sound too keen on this alternative—it is simply the way God has arranged things: "Whether the pleasure we feel in contemplating beautiful objects may have any necessary connection with the belief of their excellence, or whether that pleasure be conjoined with this belief by the good pleasure only of our Maker, I will not determine."[11]

Fortunately, with a modern understanding of evolution, we should be able to resume Reid's inquiry with more confidence than he himself could muster. Here are certain questions, raised by his analysis, to which we might hope to give scientific answers:

- What kind of emotion is the "agreeable emotion" aroused by beauty? Allowing that the experience may be more or less intense, what makes our response to beauty the same emotion in different cases?
- What kind of excellence gives things the "amiable quality" that we call beautiful? Allowing again for different degrees, what are the markers of excellence that make it the same quality across different examples?
- Assuming there is indeed a causal link between our judging something excellent in this way and feeling this emotion, how has this evolved by natural selection? What exactly have been the survival benefits on which selection has operated?

* * *

I am going to concentrate on four domains of human life where we regularly rely on judgments of beauty to determine our life choices:

- *Personal beauty:* The beauty of bodies and minds that indicate good health and character in another person
- *Structural beauty:* The beauty of procedures, tools, and structures that do their job well
- *Environmental beauty:* The beauty of places that offer us opportunities to flourish
- *Cognitive beauty:* The beauty of patterns that help guide our minds to make sense of the world

I show how humans, by following beauty's lead, can gain a variety of material and psychological rewards. Insofar as these rewards contribute to biological survival, we should have no difficulty in explaining how "the human sense of beauty" could have been favored by natural selection.

And yet the very diversity of the examples may present a problem for an evolutionary account. For how can we investigate "the" sense of beauty when it apparently takes so many forms? Even if we use the same word from one case to the next—beautiful faces, beautiful houses, beautiful hand axes, beautiful trees, beautiful music, even beautiful morals—do we mean the same thing by it? Or is this simply a way of talking, a linguistic convention that has no scientific basis? It is important to show that the things we call beautiful not only have objective features in common but also evoke in us a similar subjective emotion.

* * *

I take the line, agreed with by many critics, that beauty is a *formal* quality. It arises not from what a thing is *made of* but from the way its parts are *observably related*. The German philosopher Johann Herbart, for example, wrote in 1808: "The conclusion is that each element of the approved or distasteful whole is, in isolation, indifferent; in a word, the material is indifferent, but the form comes under the aesthetic judgement. . . . Those judgements which are commonly conceived under the name of taste are the result of the perfect apprehension of relations formed by a complexity of elements."[12]

But it's one thing to recognize that what matters is formal structural relationships, another to say what exactly these are, and another to say why. The poet Gerard Manley Hopkins is almost alone in having proposed a specific theory. "All beauty," he wrote in a student essay in 1865, "may by a metaphor be called rhyme."[13] I take up this suggestion and make the analysis of *rhyme* the backbone of this book. I discuss what rhyme amounts to, the many guises that it takes, how humans (and other creatures) detect and respond to it, and why it is often an indicator of "real excellence" from the standpoint of biological survival.

To anticipate how this plays out in the chapters to come, let me flag some of the possible benefits of seeking out rhyme:

- *Personal rhyme:* When another person has bodily features that rhyme, they are likely to possess traits that are desirable in a partner or friend. When they act in ways that rhyme, speak in ways that rhyme, create works of art that rhyme, and so on, the same applies.
- *Structural rhyme:* When structures such as a bridge or building are made of rhyming parts, they are likely to be relatively strong and resilient. The same goes for utensils, tools, and all things made for practical use. Rhyme also enhances "tools of thought."
- *Environmental rhyme:* When a natural landscape contains rhyming geographical features, rhyming plants, and rhyming animals, it is likely to be a good place for humans to settle. This is equally so if a civic landscape contains rhyming monuments and architecture.
- *Cognitive rhyme:* When a cognitively challenging situation exhibits rhyming patterns, it is likely to offer an opportunity for deeper understanding.

The first three of these benefits are real and important and go some way to explaining why people's love of rhyme has evolved. But I argue that the benefit of being attracted to cognitive rhyme is fundamental. It came first in evolution and underlies everything else. In fact, this is the reason that the shape and dynamics of the aesthetic emotion are remarkably similar across different domains. In particular, there's the feeling that beauty brings closure, that this is how things *ought* to be. I focus on the sense of "oughtness" and the special feeling it arouses.

A beautiful poem, a smiling baby, a flower garden, a sunset, a mathematical equation, the body of a dancer, a Greek temple, a reciprocating steam engine: They all can seem in their own way *perfect*. But the semimoral emotion this arouses is notably absent in the case of objects that are merely attractive without being beautiful—a pile of banknotes, a Christmas pudding, or a vacant parking space.

What does it mean that a perceived arrangement is how it ought to be? The art historian Ernst Gombrich, taking the perspective of an artist engaged in *making* a work of beauty, observed: "What an artist worries about as he plans his pictures, makes his sketches, or wonders whether he has completed his canvas, is . . . whether he has got it 'right.'"[14] I argue that the appreciation of beauty in general is the other side of this same coin. Knowingly or not, we take what I call "the artistic stance"—implicitly considering how a thing has been created and whether it has been "got right."

* * *

If I'm correct about these similarities in the way people recognize and respond to beauty across domains, we'll have found strong support for the idea that evolved mechanisms of the human brain underlie the response to beauty.

But this brings on another objection that I should deal with straight away. If there is an evolved "beauty center" in the human brain, why is there so much variation between individuals? How can we talk about "the" human brain in matters of taste if, as is generally acknowledged, everyone is a law unto themselves? The point was forcefully made by Maureen Duffy in her review of Jane Goodall's book *In the Shadow of Man*. Goodall had written, "But what if a chimpanzee wept tears when he heard Bach thundering from a cathedral organ?," to which Duffy replied, "What indeed if an Amazon pigmy or a 19th century factory hand wept tears at such a minority western cultural phenomenon?"[15]

Many commentators have taken the diversity of human tastes (especially attitudes to high art) to mean that the idea of "an instinctive sense of beauty" is a nonstarter. However, the significance of individual variation should not be overplayed. While it's true that there are cross-cultural differences in what people find beautiful and the ways they respond, this is not inconsistent with the sense of beauty having a genetic basis in the human brain. Reid himself suggested that, for animals, the sense of beauty will "in each species be adapted to its manner of life." For nonhuman animals, this generally means being adapted to just one manner of life, but for humans, the options have been left much more open. Humans are, by nature, shape-shifters, with an exceptional ability to make the best of different cultural and environmental circumstances.

We should not be surprised if, even with a beauty instinct, people still may have to learn what's beautiful *for them*, just as with a language instinct, they have to learn the grammar and vocabulary of the language spoken in their neighborhood. Furthermore, they may need *to get their eye in*. Think of how you yourself have failed to appreciate a work of art simply because you didn't—yet—have the conceptual tools to understand it.

On top of this, we might expect differences in the way people *use* beauty for their own purposes, just as in the way they *use* morality. In this regard, I would point to a further source of variation within a culture. It's that aesthetic choices by humans are not necessarily private matters. The expression of taste can become a badge by which individuals deliberately express conformity or nonconformity. For some, departing from the cultural norm becomes a statement of their individuality.

This is all to say that an "objective theory" of the origins of beauty does not have to imply that one size fits all.

* * *

The exposition of these ideas about rhyme and its ramifications takes up most of the book. Only in the final chapter do I move to the question of the *abundance* of beauty in our world: why we encounter so much of it apparently awaiting our attention; why, indeed, the world's beauty—the amount of rhyme—has been accumulating as time goes by.

What emerges is a new synthesis: that the argument from design and the argument from beauty come down to one and the same scientific truth. The laws of nature have designed the world we live in, it's the nature of these laws to generate a world that's full of rhyme, it's because the world rhymes that we can make sense of it, and it's because we can make sense of it that we can live.

2 THE CAT SAT ON THE MAT

The phrase is peculiarly satisfying: "The cat sat on the mat." "The cat sat on the sofa" doesn't hit the same spot, nor, for that matter, does "The cat sat on the cat."

Rhyming sounds are an elementary example of a beautiful arrangement. The sounds "cat" and "mat" go together, enhance each other, complete each other, bring about closure. The satisfaction we feel in this simple relationship is hard to describe. It isn't exactly sensory (though it is mediated via our sense organs), and it isn't exactly intellectual (though it does involve comparison and memory). To put it grandly, we delight in the fact that two sounds that deserve each other have met up because of our attention. And it's not only sounds. As we'll see, there can be rhymes in other sensory modalities. Colors can rhyme, smells can, feelings can, perhaps ideas can.

What's going on?

If you search for a scientific explanation of why people like rhymes, you'll find almost nothing worth having. You won't even find a good analysis of how rhyme can be defined. It's surely surprising that such an in-your-face psychological phenomenon—and something so intimately connected to beauty—should have sparked so little inquiry.

The exception is the remarkable essay by Gerard Manley Hopkins that I referred to previously: "On the Origin of Beauty: A Platonic Dialogue." He wrote it for his tutor when he was an undergraduate at Balliol College, Oxford, aged twenty. I first came across it when I was a newly appointed lecturer at Oxford in the late 1960s and had just begun research into evolutionary aesthetics. It felt as if the sun had come out from behind a cloud.

To launch the present discussion, I shall let Hopkins set out the argument himself (here highly condensed). The original runs to fourteen thousand words—some student essay![1]

* * *

Hopkins casts his piece in the form of a Platonic dialogue between a professor and a student named Hanbury in an Oxford college garden (with the student playing the role of the "Yes, Socrates, how clever of you" patsy). The two of them discuss the beauty of the garden, and they dwell in particular on the leaves of a chestnut tree. (Figure 2.1 shows a picture of the fan I picked from a tree in the same garden.) They also encounter an artist named Middleton who contributes to the discussion.

The professor holds forth on the structural relations within the fan, pointing out how each leaf is a variation with a difference of the common pattern and how the overall shape of the fan shows mirror symmetry, the left half being a perfect reflection of the right. In other ways, the internal reflections are tantalizingly irregular. The two horizontal leaves are mirror images, but each of the large oblique leaves is reflected by

FIGURE 2.1
The chestnut fan. Photo by the author.

a copy of itself in miniature, and the large central leaf has no counterpart at all.

He remarks too on the relation between the leaves of the chestnut and the leaves of other trees, drawing attention to the way in which the chestnut leaf, being fatter at the distal than the central end, is the opposite shape to the common shape shown, say, by the leaf of a lime tree.

The professor continues:

> "Then the beauty of the oak and the chestnut-fan and the sky is a mixture of likeness and difference or agreement and disagreement or consistency and variety or symmetry and change."
>
> "It seems so, yes."
>
> "And if we did not feel the likeness we should not feel them so beautiful, or if we did not feel the difference we should not feel them so beautiful. The beauty we find is from the comparison we

make of the things with themselves, seeing their likeness and difference, is it not?"

Before long, they move on to the subject of poetry, embodying rhythm and rhyme:

"You think these things beautiful, do you not, rhythm, and rhyme?"

"Of course I do; everybody does."

"And what is rhythm? Is it not the repetition of a regular sequence of syllables either in accent or quantity? . . . These sequences are technically called feet. The repetition of them makes language rhythmical."

DUM da / DUM da / DUM da / DUM. Take this verse of Percy Bysshe Shelley's, the professor suggests [I've added slashes to mark the feet]:

Music/ when sweet/ voices/ die
Vibrates/ in the/ memor/y
Odours/ when sweet/ violets/ sicken
Live with/in the/ sense they/ quicken.

. . .

"The accentual sequence . . . in *odours* is the same as in *when sweet* or in *sicken,* but the foot is not exactly like them simply because it is made of a different word. . . . It has the same sequence of accentuation, but illustrated in different syllables. Rhythm therefore is likeness tempered with difference, is it not?"

"Yes, it is so. How could I not see that?"

"And the beauty of rhythm is traced to the same causes as that of the chestnut-fan, is it not so?"

"Yes, it is." . . .

"What is rhyme," said the Professor. "Is it not agreement of sound?"

"With a slight disagreement, yes," broke in Hanbury. . . .

"Yes," said Middleton. "In fact it seems to me rhyme is the epitome of your principle. All beauty may by a metaphor be called rhyme, may it not?"

"Indeed," says the Professor. . . . "Beauty therefore is a relation, and the apprehension of it a comparison. The sense of beauty in fact is a comparison, is it not?"

"So it would appear."

* * *

Hopkins's theory of beauty is unashamedly cerebral. He argues that we find an object beautiful as and when we discern the existence of formal relationships within and without, patterns of assonance and dissonance. The metaphor he settles on is the sounds of poetry—verbal rhythm and rhyme. But the relationship of "likeness tempered with difference" transcends sensory modalities. There will be the opportunity for us to notice it whenever we perceive things as being *of a kind*. And when we do, we will feel the telltale emotion that comes with realizing how things *connect*: "That's beautiful," "That's how it ought to be."

Fifty years later, the art critic Clive Bell wrote:

> If we can discover some quality common and peculiar to all the objects that provoke [the aesthetic emotion], we shall have solved what I take to be the central problem of aesthetics. . . . What quality, is shared by all objects that provoke our aesthetic emotions? What quality is common to Santa Sophia and the windows at Chartres, Mexican sculpture, a Persian bowl, Chinese carpets, Giotto's frescoes at Padua, and the masterpieces of Poussin, Piero della Francesca, and Cézanne? Only one answer seems possible—significant form. In each, lines and colours combined in a particular way, certain forms and relations of forms.[2]

Yet Bell, by his own admission, is vague about what exactly "significant form" amounts to—"lines and colours combined in a particular way, certain forms and relations of forms." You'll know it when you see it! Hopkins, on the other hand, has been precise. Only one answer seems possible—rhyme.

So has Hopkins solved the central problem of aesthetics? He himself recognizes his theory is not complete. At one point, the student objects that the professor's theory seems rather inhuman and mathematical: "I am sure there is in the higher forms of beauty—at least I seem to feel—something mystical, something I don't know how to call it. Is not there now something beyond what you have explained?"

The professor decides this is the moment to break off for a cup of tea. However, when they return to the discussion, he continues to insist that it's all about structure. He suggests the additional quality—that may or not be present—derives from the "structural unity" that exists when a thing of beauty fits within a larger whole. Thus, for example, the beauty of each separate verse of William Shakespeare's *Romeo and Juliet* is enhanced by its place within the play, further enhanced by this play's place among Shakespeare's tragedies, further by the tragedies' place beside the comedies and histories, etc.

The student grudgingly buys into this answer. But I have to say, if I had been in his place, I would have felt shortchanged. While the professor may have a point, it would seem to be more of the same cool logic, when he has been asked for something beyond this—perhaps something that speaks more to specifically human interests. As we develop our evolutionary inquiry, I hope a different level of answer will emerge, even as we stay within the framework of Hopkins's formal theory.

Nonetheless, let's agree that at the very least Hopkins has got us off to a good start. What impressed me when I first read the essay was how he had discovered a way of deconstructing beauty that, so far as it goes, is remarkably applicable in practice. I've gone on to find that, again and again, when I have been taken by the beauty of a landscape or a musical composition or a painting or a set of ideas—without immediately knowing quite what it is about it that works so well—I've been able to see on reflection how it involves internal rhymes (that presumably I've discerned prereflectively). Aha, so that's what's going on!

In chapter 4, I shall walk you through a gallery of examples of rhyme in art and nature to illustrate how widely true it is that rhyme in many different guises is considered beautiful by human beings.

But before going there, I want to propose a more systematic typology of rhyme than Hopkins gave us. So first, a short chapter about definition.

3 LIKENESS AND DIFFERENCE

As a definition of rhyme, "likeness tempered with difference" is wide open to interpretation. What sort of likeness? What sort of difference? Just how much likeness is required, and how much difference is tolerable?

I shall define rhyme broadly, in terms of *family relationship*. Two entities, A and B, rhyme when we recognize that, while they differ, they belong together. I'll focus on two types of belonging.

With what I'll call "symmetrical rhyme" (figure 3.1), we recognize that A and B belong together because we see how they are generically *the same kind of thing*. Typically, this comes about when A and B have some "essential property" in common, while they differ in respect of some "contingent property." This means that they can be regarded as transforms of each other. Thus, in figure 3.1 the essential property common to A and B in every case is the shape of the jagged edge. The various contingent properties are (i) size, (ii) color, (iii) vertical rotation, (iv) horizontal mirror rotation.

Note that A can *become* B by being translated in time or space, rotated, grown, shrunk, recolored, flipped, and so on.

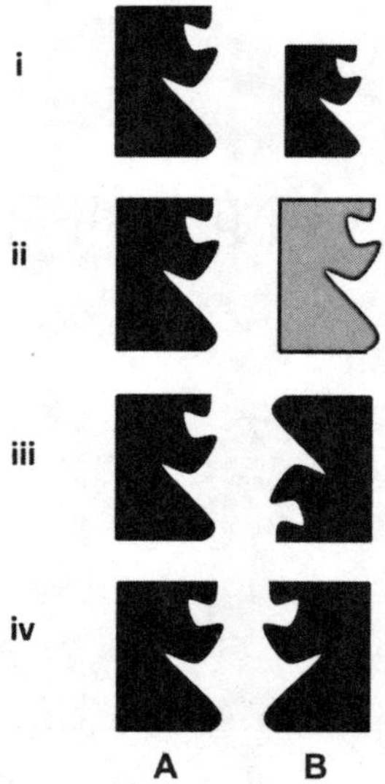

FIGURE 3.1
Symmetrical rhyme. Drawings by the author.

In general, A can become B by a simple operation that does not change its nature but substitutes A's contingent property by B's contingent property.

By contrast, with what I'll call "reciprocal rhyme" (figure 3.2), we recognize that A and B belong together not because they are the same kind of thing but because they are a *good fit* for each other. Typically, this comes about when they have

FIGURE 3.2
Reciprocal rhyme. Drawing by the author.

properties that reciprocate or answer to each other, so that they fit together as lock and key. Thus, in figure 3.2, the shape of A's jagged edge is the exact inverse of B's. This means they can interdigitate, but there's no simple way A can be rotated or flipped to become B. A is conventionally called female and B male, and their gender is not negotiable.

We'll see shortly how, with these two categories of rhyme, we can capture most if not all of the rhyming phenomena that people find beautiful. But first, to show how the definitions work, here are some elementary examples.

SYMMETRICAL RHYME (ESSENTIAL LIKENESS, CONTINGENT DIFFERENCE):

- *Rhyming words:* E.g., "Cat" and "mat." The essential property is "how the word ends," and the contingent property is "how it begins."
- *Prime numbers:* E.g., numbers "17" and "23." The essential property is "being divisible only by 1 and itself," and the contingent property is "itself."
- *First cousins:* E.g., Charles Darwin and Emma Darwin. The essential property is "having the same grandparents but different parents," and the contingent property is "the parents."
- *Yourself at different ages:* E.g., ages "twenty-one" and "forty-five." The essential property is "your personal identity," and the contingent property is "your age."
- *Harmonic musical notes:* E.g., "middle C" and "upper C." The essential property is "the fundamental frequency," and the contingent property is the multiple of this frequency."
- *Anagrams:* E.g., "asleep" and "please." The essential property is "a word made of the same set of letters," and the contingent property is "the order of the letters."

RECIPROCAL RHYME (INVERSE LIKENESS, GOOD FIT):

- *A complementary marriage:* E.g., "Jack Sprat" and "his wife"
- *A container and its contents:* E.g., "a sheath" and "a dagger"
- *A stamp and its impression:* E.g., "an engraved plate" and "the print"
- *Predator and prey:* E.g., "an owl" and "a mouse"
- *Question and answer:* E.g., "Who killed Cock Robin?" and "'I,' said the sparrow."

HYBRID RHYME (SYMMETRY AND RECIPROCITY COMBINED):

- *Yin and yang:* The shapes both resemble and answer each other (figure 3.3).
- *The nurse and her patient:* The nurse rotated becomes her complement—the grumpy patient in her care (figure 3.4).

FIGURE 3.3
Yin and yang. Traditional symbol.

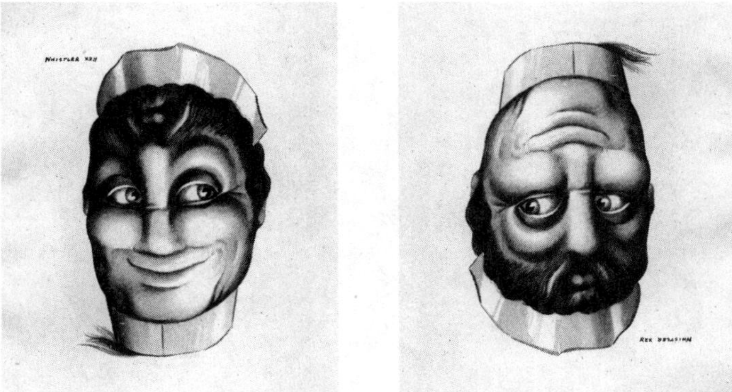

FIGURE 3.4
"Nurse? Quite the reverse!" From *OHO!*, by Laurence Whistler and Rex Whistler, 1946. London: John Lane & the Bodley Head. In the public domain.

4 A GALLERY OF RHYME

Here are examples of rhyming beauty, in no particular order. I'd like you to have that "Aha!" feeling.

THE LILIES OF THE FIELD

"Consider the lilies of the field, how they grow; they toil not, neither do they spin: And yet I say unto you, That even Solomon in all his glory was not arrayed like one of these" (Matthew 6:28–29, King James version) (figure 4.1).

Gerard Manley Hopkins chose the leaves of a tree to illustrate his thesis on the origin of beauty. But he might have done better to give the example of flowers.

Consider first the static form of a simple flower such as a primrose. The flower head consists of petals arranged in radial symmetry around a cluster of stamens, and it is carried on a stalk that bears a set of leaves. Petals, stamens, and leaves form three sets of contrasting rhyming elements. Each petal differs in detail from the other members of its set and yet shares their distinctive shape and color, and the same is true for the

FIGURE 4.1
Anemones de Caen (Gallilean "lilies of the field"). Photo by the author.

stamens and the leaves. The features that unite each set at the same time separate one set from another.

Then consider the flower's kinetic form. The living flower is in a continual state of growth, changing its form from day to day. The transformations that occur as the flower buds, blossoms, and decays give rise to a temporal structure in which each successive form rhymes with the preceding one.

Third, consider groups of flowers. Typically, each flowering plant bears several blooms, and plants of the same species tend to grow in close proximity, so that various related blooms are on show together.

Furthermore, groups of flowers of different species commonly grow alongside one another—daisies and buttercups beside each other in the field, violets and primroses together in the hedgerow. So while the flowers of one species rhyme with each other, the rhyme is given added poignancy by the contrasting rhymes of different species.

BIRDS IN FLIGHT

Flowers showcase the modular design that characterizes living things. Plants and animals are built on the principle of replication—at one level, replication of structural elements within a single body and, at another, replication of the body of the organism as a whole. But at either level, the replicas are seldom, if ever, perfect copies. They are variations on a theme.

The same goes for animal behavior. Louis Halle, the American naturalist, described his pleasure in seeing kittiwake seabirds in the air: "The pulsating flight of the kittiwake combines irregularity with regularity in the way that distinguishes everything in nature from anything that is merely mechanical. . . . I never saw a kittiwake fly in a perfectly straight line, even when purposefully maintaining a single direction. Instead, there is a slight wavering or yawing that goes with a habit of tilting from side to side. The wingbeats have a regular rhythm within which they are irregular. The tilting and wavering is accompanied by an alternate quickening and retardation of the beat, but all within the limits of the measure" (figure 4.2).[1]

Halle quotes the painter Auguste Renoir: "The Earth is not round. An orange is not round. None of its segments has either the same form or the same weight. Open them and they will not have the same number of seeds, and the seeds will not be alike." Yet what makes the seeds or the segments *rhyme* is that they are alike even while they differ.

FIGURE 4.2
Aaron Boughtflower, *Kittiwake Flight Study*, pencil, 2022. © Aaron Boughtflower. By kind permission of the artist.

CLOUDS

Modularity is not restricted to living things. Whole landscapes tend to be shaped by geological forces into "modular" forms, with fractal versions appearing at different scales. Mountains, lakes, rivers, sand dunes, snow crystals, pebbles, raindrops, ocean waves: Each is alike but different from its relatives (figure 4.3).

Clouds are a wonderful example of modularity. For reasons that are only partially understood by meteorologists, clouds fall into distinct types. While there's an unlimited range of possible states for a parcel of air (considering variables of temperature, pressure, humidity, and so on), certain combinations of these variables just happen to be more stable than others.

FIGURE 4.3
Clouds. Fair Weather Forms. Anonymous engraving, c. 1880. Public domain.

These stable states correspond to the kinds of clouds we recognize and name—such as cumulus, stratus, and cirrus.

Different types of cloud tend to occupy different areas of the sky. Within these areas, they individuate to form separate masses with quite sharp edges. Where the wet cloud consisting of tiny water droplets comes up against relatively dry air, any droplets that escape immediately evaporate, thus opening an empty space between one cloud and the next. From our human perspective, looking up from the ground, there arise families of individual clouds floating across the sky. Instead of what might have been a fog, we are presented with an aerial poem.

THE RAINBOW

The rainbow is the poster boy of natural beauty. It hangs in the air as a perfectly formed arc of light, contrasting with the irregular shapes of the landscape and the clouds it overlays.

It's as if nature is asserting the triumph of order over chaos. And some order! The bow is made up of seven rhyming bands of color—red, orange, yellow, green, blue, indigo, and violet—nestled alongside one another. Sometimes there will be a secondary rainbow outside the main one—and the order of the colors of this bow will be reversed (figure 4.4).

Rainbows are an illusion. There's nothing out there in the sky that is made of colored stripes. There are only falling raindrops diffracting the sun's light. As Hopkins himself remarked in an early poem: "The rainbow shines, but only in the thought / Of him that looks."[2] And yet rainbows are not *unreal*. They show up in photographs. Other people are able to see the same bow you do.

While it lasts, every rainbow has a singular identity. Like the oak tree on the horizon, it's *this* rainbow. In another respect, it's quite unlike the oak tree, because its properties depend on

FIGURE 4.4

Landscape with Large Rainbow. Engraving after Peter Paul Rubens, c. 1638. Public domain.

where you, the observer, are located. When you and I look at the "same" rainbow from different viewpoints, we'll each see it as touching the ground at a different place. Rainbows play games with us: Catch me if you can.

CYCLIC NUMBERS

Mathematics is riddled with rhyme and rhythm. The reciprocal of the number 7 is 0.142857142857142857 (or 0.142857 recurring). But the number 142857 rhymes on another level too. If you multiply it first by 1, then by 2, then by 3, and so on seven times, you get the sequence below. Six cycling numbers and then the unexpected ending:

142857

285714

428571

571428

714285

857142

999999

My grandfather had a hand-cranked calculating machine on which I would try this out over and again (half hoping to catch it making a mistake). The calculator produced a satisfying crunch as numbers slotted into place. Years later, I came across a proof that every number system—not only the decimal system—must have at least one cyclic number like this.

THE GOLDEN SECTION

As ancient philosophers discovered, any straight line can be divided into two parts such that the ratio of the longer part, x, to the shorter part, *y*, is equal to the ratio of the whole length to the longer part. Thus, in the example below, $x/y = (x + y)/x$:

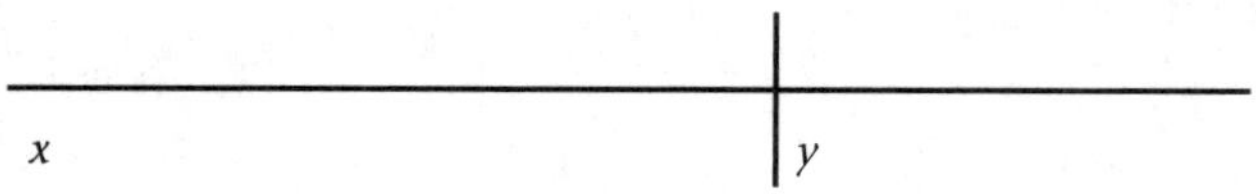

This ratio, 1.618, is the "golden section." Historically, this ratio has often been considered to represent the perfect balance between more and less. The architect Le Corbusier developed an entire system of design proportions based on it that he called the "Modulor."

In recent years, psychologists who study aesthetics have been reluctant to admit that the golden section has any special claim to beauty. As Christopher McManus has pointed out, this is largely because they have not been able to *explain* it: "There is a dearth of psychological *theory* as to *why* the golden section might have any role."[3]

Yet look how it ties in with rhyme. First, construct a golden rectangle *a*, with sides proportionate to the golden section (figure 4.5). Divide this into a square on the left and a smaller rectangle *b* on the right, and *b* will itself be a golden rectangle. Do this again to *b*, and it will make another still smaller golden rectangle *c*. And so on, to generate a chain of rhyming rectangles, alike in shape but different in size.

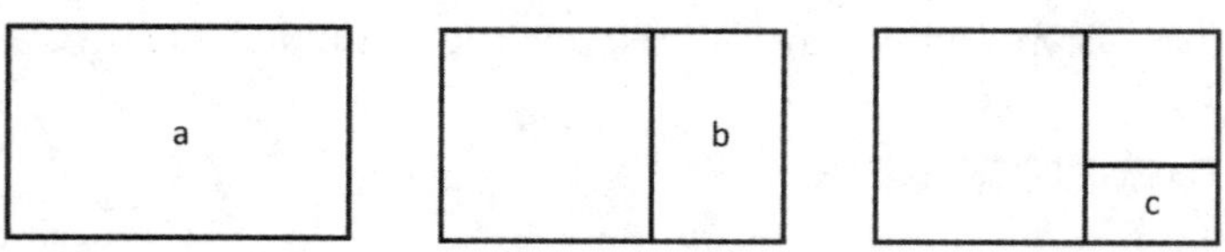

FIGURE 4.5
Golden rectangles. Drawings by the author.

A spiral can be drawn through this sequence of rectangles (the Fibonacci spiral, figure 4.6). As it happens, this is exactly the same spiral that shows up in the seedhead of a sunflower, a pinecone, a head of broccoli—or the arrangement of leaves growing around the main stem of a plant, positioned so as to capture the most sunlight (an unexpected nod to utility).

THE PIANO SONATA

Among the arts, music has traditionally been the medium for the purest expression of abstract structural relations. And "likeness tempered with difference" is the stock-in-trade of every musical composer. The composer presents, say, a simple melody, repeats it a few times, and then launches into a series of variations by playing it in a different key, with a different emphasis, or on a different instrument, eventually returning to the original. But repetition of the same theme, albeit with variations, becomes in the long run relatively dull. As in poetry, contrast is needed to bring home the unity of the

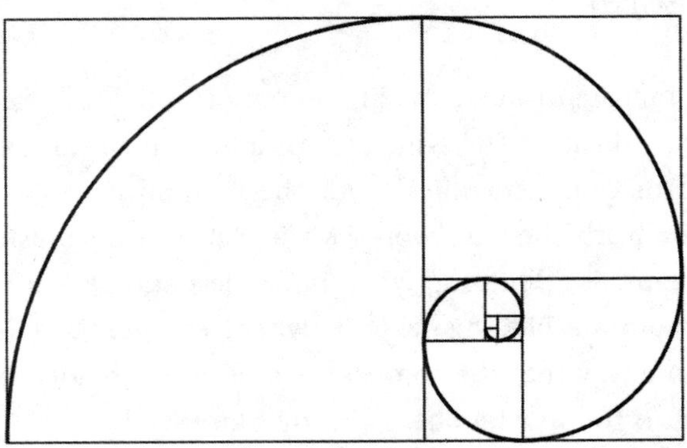

FIGURE 4.6
The Fibonacci spiral. Drawing by the author.

rhyming elements, and the composer typically introduces a contrasting theme with its own variations.

Thus, a simple piece such as a nocturne by Frédéric Chopin has the following structure—two distinct themes, A and B, arranged as AABBA. Taking his nocturne in E flat as an example, the first tune is repeated twice to establish the main key and the main subject matter in the memory of the hearer. Then comes the second tune, which is in the most nearly related key (so that the effect of the contrast is not lost because of too great dissimilarity). Then the two tunes alternate, with small changes introduced at each repetition in the form of, for instance, decorative arabesques in the right-hand part while the left hand's chords provide reciprocal support.

In more complex pieces, such as sonatas by Ludwig van Beethoven, the composer introduces a "development" section where the motifs of the first theme are picked up and rearranged until, just at the point where the hearer may be in danger of losing track of what is going on, order is restored by the "recapitulation" of the first theme pure and simple.

PHILOSOPHY

As he prepared to take his life by poison, Socrates recalled a recurring dream: "The same dream came to me sometimes in one form, and sometimes in another, but always saying the same or nearly the same words: Make and cultivate music, said the dream. . . . [Philosophy] is the noblest and best of music. The dream was bidding me to do what I was already doing, in the same way that the competitor in a race is bidden by the spectators to run when he is already running."[4]

Philosophy at every level relies on symmetries and reciprocity. Even a simple syllogism has a rhyming structure: "All men are mortal. Socrates is a man. Socrates is mortal." It's a kind of logical sonata: AB, CA, CB.

WORDPLAY AND ANALOGY

Words can rhyme even when they have no meaning. Lewis Carroll's nonsense poem "Jabberwocky" is a delightful example. Here is how it starts.

> 'Twas brillig, and the slithy toves
> Did gyre and gimble in the wabe;
> All mimsy were the borogoves,
> And the mome raths outgrabe.[5]

The shape of the verse draws attention to words that are alike but different in their sounds, so that they rhyme acoustically. Although there's nothing to suggest any deeper resemblance—"toves" and "borogroves" don't refer to the same thing under a different name—the verse is remarkably pleasing and memorable.

The complement of this is when two things are paired that are physically quite different but nonetheless have an abstract property in common so that they rhyme semantically: "He fought like a lion." Now we're into the realm of *analogies*. And analogies can be pleasing and also deeply revealing: "Gas molecules are like billiard balls," "Time is like a river," "Death is like eternal sleep," "Light is like a wave." Or, a literary example, "[Mark Antony's] delights were dolphin-like; they showed his back above the element they lived in."

The power of analogy lies in providing insightful comparisons that can be played with and enjoyed without any constraining commitment to physical identity. Time is not a river—but it flows like one. Gas molecules are not billiard balls—but they bounce off each other as if they were.

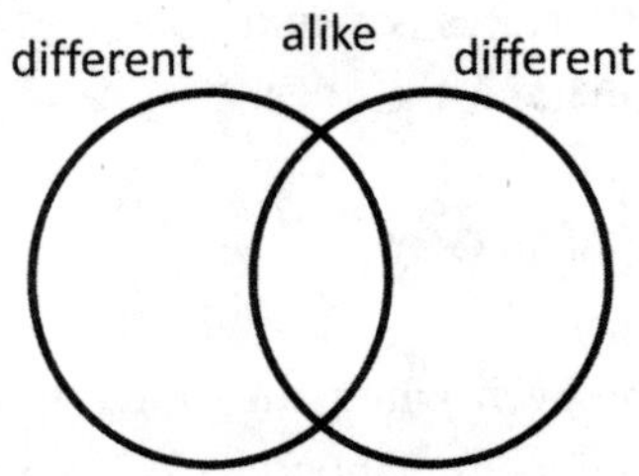

FIGURE 4.7
A Venn diagram. Drawing by the author.

Antony was not a dolphin, but he rose above the crowd. As in a Venn diagram, analogies focus attention on a property held in common between two things by subtracting everything else—so the property can be considered on its own (figure 4.7).

WRAP-AROUND LOVE

Zora Neale Hurston, in her novel *Their Eyes Were Watching God,* wrote: "Love is lak de sea. It's uh movin' thing, but still and all, it takes its shape from de shore it meets, and it's different with every shore."[6]

Turning back to figure 1.1 of this book, think of the Turkish mother sitting on the beach, entranced by the spectacle unfolding before her. Her five children dashing through the water. The waves rhythmically rolling in and crashing on the sand. The receding expanse of grey-blue water ending at a flat horizon under the cloudy sky. Symmetries everywhere. But reciprocity too. Looking along the line of the beach, she would have seen the sea lapping the land, folding itself into rocky inlets, defining the coast of her homeland as the reverse of the ocean.

FIGURE 4.8
St. Margaret's Bay, Dover. Istock photo. Standard license.

Matthew Arnold, on Dover beach, found his way to the same analogy for wrap-around love: "The Sea of Faith / Was once, too, at the full, and round earth's shore / Lay like the folds of a bright girdle furled" (figure 4.8).[7]

RAP

The rap artist Eminem, in "Cleaning Out My Closet," sounds off about his mama:

> Bitching that someone's always going through her purse and
> shit's missing
> Going through public housing systems, victim of Münchausen's
> Syndrome.

The lyrics are a poem of sorts, and they sort of rhyme. The rhyme scheme, however, is less than obvious. The poet Alice Major explains:

> The classic definitions of rhyme require every sound after an initially different element to be the same: [b]one/[st]one, or [n]unnery/[g]unnery. The Eminem rhyme clearly flunks that test. When we map "public housin' systems" onto "Münchausen's Syndrome," there's no point where everything after an initial sound matches. So what do we hear to classify it as rhyme?
>
> The table [table 4.1] shows that we do hear nine sounds in each phrase that match up—and most importantly, they are in the same order. Order is critical. You can come up with a phrase that has the same sounds as "Münchausen's Syndrome" and yet won't rhyme: "Sixteen Zen house chums" has even more matching sounds than "public housin' systems," and even has a fairly similar pattern of strong and weak stresses. But because the order doesn't match, our ears don't register rhyme. In effect, the phrases are not the same shape.[8]

You might think that this explanation is overanalytical, a case of unweaving the rainbow. But Major's point is that this is what our brains do anyway—unweave the rhyming words.

MONET'S CATHEDRAL

Artists are unweavers and explainers. They take a slice of nature and guide us to see its secret rhymes. Émile Zola wrote of Camille Pissarro's painting of Jalais Hill (figure 4.9): "Nothing would be more banal were it not so grand. From ordinary reality the painter's temperament has drawn a rare poem of life and strength."[9]

For Wallace Stevens, "It's not every day that the world arranges itself into a poem."[10] But when it does, we may still have to wait for a painter to show it to us. Robert Browning drew attention to the artist's role:

Table 4.1
Table of rhyming elements between "publichowzinsistemz" and "munchhowzensindrem" (after Alice Major)

p	=	m
u	✓	u
b	≠	nch
lic	≠	
h	✓	h
ow	✓	ow
z	✓	z
i	≈	ə
n	✓	n
s	✓	s
i	✓	i
s	≠	
t	≠	n
	≠	dr
ə	✓	ə
m	✓	m
z	≠	

Notes: ≠ indicates there is no match at all between sounds. ✓ indicates there is an exact match between sounds. ≈ indicates sounds that match to some degree. For instance, we tend to hear "n" and "m" as similar enough to count as rhyme. ə is the schwa vowel that occurs so often in English. It's the indeterminate "uh" sound that you hear in "the." *Source:* From Alice Major, "Word Shapes and Rhymescapes: Translating Translation Symmetry into Music and Poetry," *Math Horizons* (February 2013): 22. By kind permission.

FIGURE 4.9
Camille Pissarro, *Jalais Hill*, 1867. Metropolitan Museum of Art. Wikimedia Commons.

> . . . we're made so that we love
> First when we see them painted, things we have passed
> Perhaps a hundred times nor cared to see;
> And so they are better, painted—better to us,
> Which is the same thing. Art was given for that;
> God uses us to help each other so,
> Lending our minds out.[11]

I like that phrase "lending our minds out," with its emphasis on the generosity of art. I think of Claude Monet lending his mind out as he heroically painted thirty versions of the facade of Rouen Cathedral, single-mindedly exploring rhyme across time and, in doing so, coming closer and closer to defining the essence of the cathedral (figure 4.10). He repeated the exercise with his haystacks and his waterlilies.

FIGURE 4.10
Claude Monet, six paintings of Rouen Cathedral, 1880s. Public domain.

Pablo Picasso was never so disciplined as Monet. But at one stage, he threw himself into making an extraordinary sequence of paintings that reworked Diego Velázquez's masterpiece, *Las Meninas* (figure 4.11). Picasso's fifty-eight versions play with the original—dissecting it, turning it inside out, testing its limits, reassembling it—culminating in the final version that he completed in a day (figure 4.12).[12]

"Painting is poetry," Picasso wrote, "and is always written in verse with plastic rhymes, forms that rhyme with one another or supply assonances either with other forms or with the space that surrounds them."[13]

FIGURE 4.11

Diego Velázquez, *Las Meninas* [cropped], 1656. Prado Museum, Madrid. Wikimedia Commons.

FIGURE 4.12

Pablo Picasso, *Las Meninas*, 1957. Picasso Museum, Barcelona. Photo by Ángel M. Felicísimo. Flickr Creative Commons CC BY 2.0.

RHYME, TRUTH, AND MAGIC

In *The Gay Science,* Friedrich Nietzsche attributed the origin of poetry to a primitive belief that rhythm and rhyme could confer magical powers to the words of prayers, carrying them "closer to the ears of the gods." "Even now," he observed, "the wisest among us are still occasionally fooled by rhythm—if only insofar as we sometimes feel an idea to be truer when it has a metrical form and presents itself with a divine skip, and jump."[14]

"Birds of a feather flock together" certainly has the ring of truth to it. But this could be just because we've heard it many times. Yet the "superstitious conjecture"—that sentences are truer when they rhyme—appears to hold even for unfamiliar sentences. Matthew McGlone and Jessica Tofighbakhsh tested the thesis experimentally by asking people to evaluate sayings they hadn't heard before that either rhymed or didn't rhyme.[15] They found the sayings that rhymed were consistently judged as more truthful, even when there was no difference in their meaning. For example, subjects who read the saying "Woes unite foes" rated it as more accurate on average than subjects who read "Misfortunes unite foes." Likewise, subjects who read "What sobriety conceals, alcohol reveals" rated it as more accurate than subjects who read "What sobriety conceals, alcohol unmasks."

The authors conclude: "If aphorisms are perceived as more accurate in rhyming than non-rhyming form, this would suggest that the traditional analytic distinction between a statement's 'rhyme and reason' (i.e., form and content) is not always appreciated by readers; in some circumstances, rhyme may be treated *as* reason." Alluding to John Keats's line, "Beauty is truth, truth beauty," they call this the "Keats heuristic."

The belief that rhyme has an intimate connection to truth shows up in another area of magical thinking, "sympathetic magic." Anthropologist James Frazer coined the term in *The Golden Bough* (1889) to refer to the widespread belief that things that resemble each other—that are alike but different—exert influence over each other. So, for example, actions performed on a doll can affect the person the doll resembles, for good or ill. Or, in medicine, a herb with yellow sap can cure jaundice, walnuts can strengthen the brain, phallic-shaped roots will cure male impotence, and so on.

More generally, people attribute magical properties to "coincidences." When two apparently unrelated events unexpectedly coincide in some salient feature—that is, they accidentally rhyme—it's hard to resist the idea that the occurrence was *meant* to happen that way. How come the sun and the moon subtend exactly the same angle in sky? How come the three pyramids of Giza are positioned so that they correspond exactly to the stars in Orion's belt, with their heights being correlated with the brightness of the stars?[16] How come Stephen Hawking's birthday, January 8, 1942, fell on the three hundredth anniversary of the death of Galileo?

No doubt we all have our stories to tell of coincidences that seem to cry out for a meaningful explanation. Here's a peculiar example. In 1979, I was visiting the pyramids with a friend who was working on a story about supernatural happenings in ancient Egypt. As the sun went down, I took a snapshot of her seven-year-old daughter as she jumped over a railing with the pyramids and Sphinx in the background (figure 4.13). When I saw the print, I was taken aback. It was as if fields of force emanating from the pyramids had indeed created "an assonance with the space that surrounds them"—and lifted the girl's arms.

FIGURE 4.13
Sasha. Photo by the author.

CONCEPTUAL ART

The artist Joseph Kosuth created a work he called *One and Three Chairs*. It featured a chair, a photograph of a chair, and a plaque giving the dictionary definition of a chair. This work now resides in New York's Museum of Modern Art (figure 4.14).

The philosopher Daniel Dennett carved a wooden apple from the wood of an apple tree, a wooden pear from the wood of a pear tree, a wooden medlar from the wood of a medlar tree. Then, to break the spell, he carved a wooden fig from the wood of a cherry tree.[17]

THE PERIODIC TABLE

The periodic table is a way of arranging the chemical elements that illustrates the "periodic law" discovered by the Russian

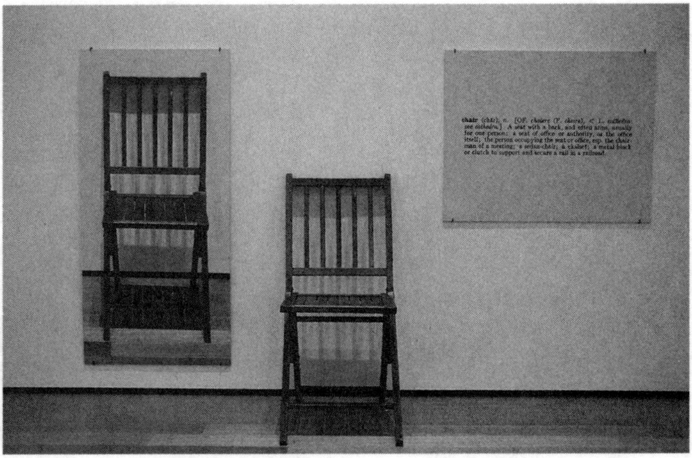

FIGURE 4.14
Joseph Kosuth, *One and Three Chairs*, 1965. Museum of Modern Art, New York. Wikimedia Commons CC BY 2.0.

scientist Dmitri Mendeleev in the 1860s (figure 4.15). The law states that a pattern emerges when the chemical elements are listed in order of their atomic weights: Elements with similar properties recur at regular intervals. This means the list can be turned into a table where elements of the same family end up above each other in a vertical column, getting heavier toward the bottom, and the families are ordered horizontally according to the element's potential for bonding, getting less reactive from left to right. Thus, the alkali and alkaline earth metals (such as sodium and calcium) are to the left, the halogens and inert gases (such as chlorine and neon) are to the right, and everything else lies in four intermediate groups in between.

Oliver Sacks described his response to this pattern when, at age twelve, he first saw it on display at the Science Museum in London:

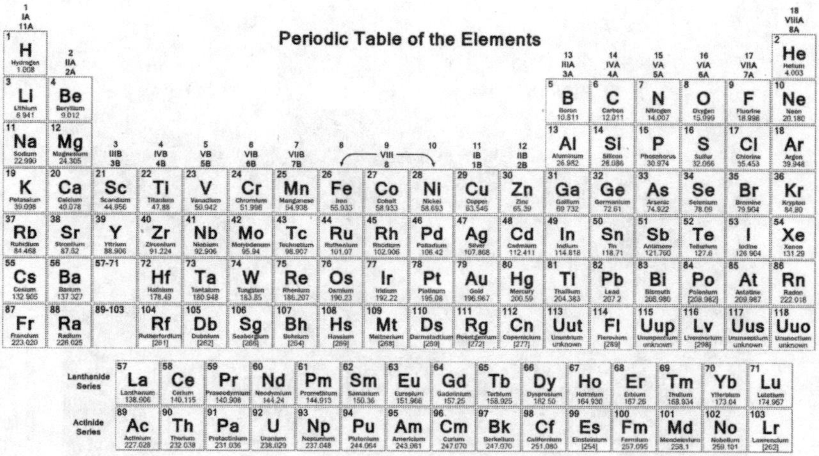

FIGURE 4.15
The periodic table of the elements showing the 118 known chemical elements. Public domain.

> The periodic table was incredibly beautiful, the most beautiful thing I had ever seen. I could never adequately analyse what I meant here by beauty—simplicity? coherence? rhythm? inevitability? Or perhaps it was the symmetry, the comprehensiveness of every element firmly locked into its place, with no gaps, no exceptions, everything implying everything else. . . . Every element echoed the properties of the one above, was a slightly heavier member of the same family. The same melody, so to speak, was played in each period—first an alkali metal, then an alkaline earth metal, then six more elements, each with its own valency or tone—but played in a different register.[18]

For the physicist Freeman Dyson, "the periodic table was a passion. . . . As a boy, I stood in front of the display for hours, thinking how wonderful it was."[19] And for Primo Levi, "Mendeleev's Periodic Table, which just during those weeks we were learning to unravel, was poetry: loftier and more solemn than

FIGURE 4.16
Hearts football club v. Celtic, 1912 Scottish Cup semifinal. Photograph from a cigarette card. Wikimedia Commons CC BY 2.0.

all the poetry we had swallowed down in liceo; and come to think of it, it even rhymed!"[20]

THE BEAUTIFUL GAME

> The game of football is like a canvas, and it's up to the players to paint the most beautiful picture. [Figure 4.16]
> —Diego Maradona

> Football is the ballet of the masses.
> —Dmitri Shostakovich

THE DOUBLE HELIX

In 1953, James Watson and Francis Crick announced that they had discovered the molecular structure of deoxyribonucleic acid (DNA). Two weeks before their paper appeared in the journal *Nature,* Crick wrote a letter to his eleven-year-old son at boarding school:[21]

My Dear Michael,

Jim Watson and I have probably made a most important discovery. We have built a model for the structure of des-oxy-ribose-nucleic-acid (read it carefully) called D.N.A. for short. . . .

Our structure is very beautiful. D.N.A. can be thought of roughly as a very long chain with flat bits sticking out. The flat bits are called the "bases." . . .

Now we have *two* of these chains winding round each other—each one is a helix—and the chain, made up of sugar and phosphorus, is on the *outside,* and the bases are all on the *inside.* I can't draw it very well, but it looks like this [figure 4.17]. . . .

The bases have names. They are Adenine, Guanine, Thymine & Cytosine. I will call them A, G, T and C. Now we find that the pairs we can make—which have one base from one chain joined to one base from another—are only A with T and G with C.

Now on one chain, as far as we can see, one can have the bases in any order, but if their order is *fixed,* then the order on the other chain is also fixed. For example, suppose the fixed chain goes: ↓ The second *must* go

A	- - - - - -	T
T	- - - - - -	A
C	- - - - - -	G
A	- - - - - -	T
G	- - - - - -	C
T	- - - - - -	A
T	- - - - - -	A

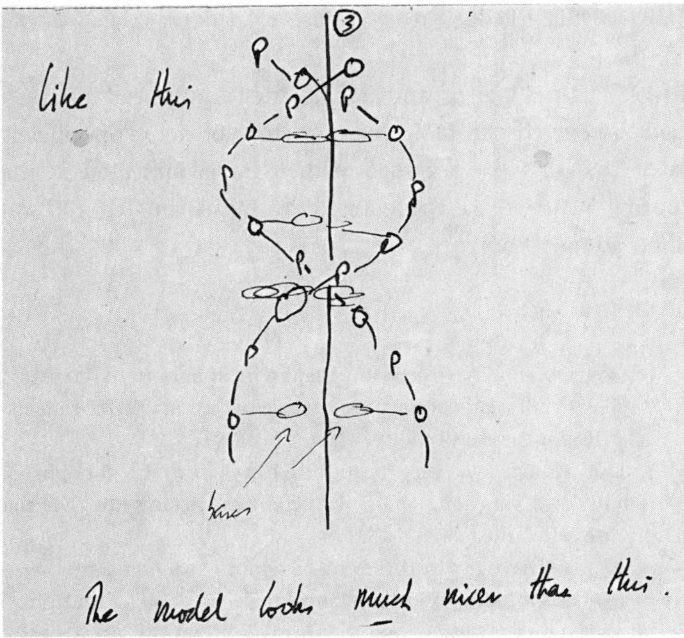

FIGURE 4.17
Francis Crick, a drawing from *Copied Letter from Francis Crick to Michael Crick*, 1953. Wellcome Collection, London, PP/CRI/D/4/3.

It is like a code. If you are given one set of letters you can write down the others.

Now we believe that the D.N.A. *is* a code. That is, the order of the bases (the letters) makes one gene different from another gene.

You can now see how Nature makes copies of the genes. . . . Because if the two chains unwind into two separate chains, and if each chain then makes another chain come together on it, then because A always goes with T, and G with C, we shall get two copies where we had one before. . . .

In other words we think we have found the basic copying mechanism by which life comes from life. . . .

Lots of love,

Daddy

Life, we may say, is rhyme all the way down.

5 REAL EXCELLENCE

If you would like to visit the gallery again, you've gotten the point. But just *why* do you find rhyme so intriguing and attractive? If the tendency to seek out rhyme and dwell on it has evolved in humans as an instinctive trait, it must be bringing us into the presence of things that somehow change our lives for the better. Is rhyme an indicator of "real excellence in the object," as Reid suggested must be true of beauty generally?

I've already named, in chapter 1, the four key domains that I think we should investigate. Of these, personal beauty, structural beauty, and environmental beauty relate to areas where humans seek out resources that directly impact their biological survival. In all three, it's fairly obvious (or will shortly become so) how rhyme could indeed be an indicator of the underlying quality of the resource. The fourth domain—cognitive beauty—is an area where the practical benefits may be harder to pin down.

The first three domains are those to which evolutionary psychologists have paid closest attention and about which most has been written. I am going to treat them only briefly in the next two chapters, not because they are not important but because (as I'll argue later) I don't believe they are of primary importance to *aesthetics*. Moreover, I do not have much new to say about them, though I do have something. As you'll have gathered, it's cognitive beauty that most interests me in the long run.

PERSONAL BEAUTY: THE BEAUTY OF PEOPLE

Humans, more than any other animal, depend for their happiness and success in life on whom of their own species they choose to associate with. Therefore, if natural selection has done its job, we can expect humans to have instinctive preferences for the company of other individuals who are likely to make particularly good mates, friends, or collaborators.

What particular bodily and mental qualities go with this? The answers may be different for reproductive partners and for other sorts of friends. Mates for breeding should be of the opposite sex, while helpers may be of either. Mates should show unequivocal signs of genetic quality, while helpers' genes may be less important. Mates should be young and fertile, while friends can be old and wise. But in most other respects, the desirable traits are going to be similar. Whatever the context, we will do well to associate with other individuals who are clever, healthy, strong, generous, trustworthy, kind, wealthy, and not too different from ourselves.

So we'll have evolved to find *external bodily markers* of these traits attractive and to be good at recognizing them. Moreover, insofar as we can, we'll have evolved to display such markers on our own bodies and to be good at advertising them. However, "insofar as we can" is an important caveat. The markers must be "honest signals" that are genuinely correlated with the traits and difficult to fake. Natural selection will have ensured, for example, that signs of trustworthiness are hard to simulate and signs of ill health hard to hide.

Where, then, can we look for reliable evidence that another person possesses the underlying physiological and mental traits that we would hope for in a partner? The answer, as it turns out, is "all over the place." The desirable qualities may be marked in individuals' physiques—their face, their bodily contours, their strength, their grace. In their skill as performers—dancing, singing, playing the flute. In the things they make—a hand axe, a necklace, a painting, a pot, a poem. In the ways they act toward others—their kindness, their wit, their gamesmanship.

In every sphere, a central feature will be rhyming beauty. To start with bodily markers, Leonardo da Vinci, taking his cue from the Roman architect Vitruvius, drew the ideal human body perfectly disposed within a circle, with proportions conforming to the golden ratio (figure 5.1). He may have been stretching a point, but there's no question people are attracted to other individuals whose bodies are balanced and symmetrical.

There is a good physiological reason that a liking for bodily balance is adaptive. Balanced individuals are likely to be those who have been particularly fortunate in their childhood development, either genetically or environmentally. Human bodies are *programmed* to display symmetry in many respects. But near-perfect symmetry can be achieved in practice only if the individual has had an exceptionally smooth ride during development. Perturbations arising for whatever reason—toxins, parasites, infection, poor diet, rogue genes, or inbreeding—are all likely to lead to an imbalance in growth that shows up on the surface, being particularly noticeable in paired structures such as the eyes and ears. These stressors can

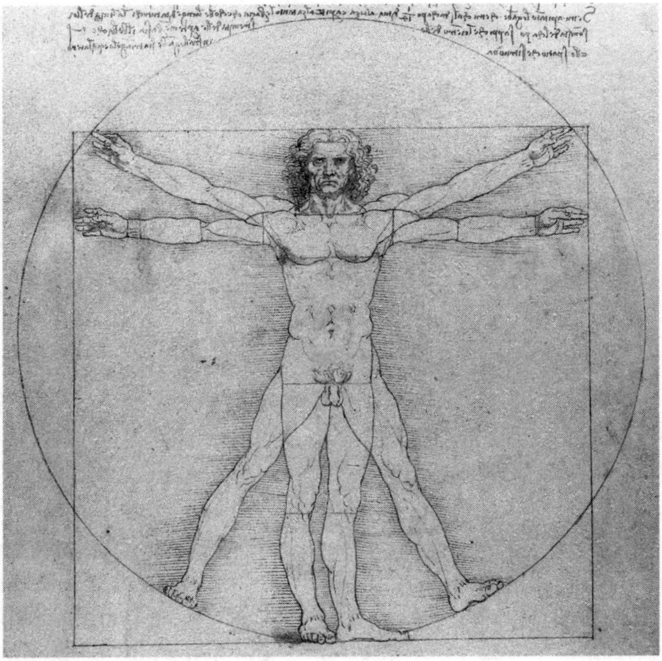

FIGURE 5.1
Leonardo da Vinci, *Vitruvian Man*, ink and watercolor drawing, c. 1490. Gallerie dell'Accademia, Venice. Public domain.

also cause lasting damage to the workings of body's immune system, vital organs, and the brain.

The upshot is that the body (especially the face) is a display board on which are written telltale clues to a person's developmental history. Thus, as a general rule (though certainly not a hard and fast one), if we are looking for a partner who is healthy in body and mind, we should prefer someone who *looks* the part. We have, in fact, evolved to be very quick to read the signs and draw conclusions. We can take in facial features in a few seconds and form lasting—and surprisingly accurate—impressions of a person's general health, self-esteem, and trustworthiness.

But we often have more than snapshots to go on. We also can look for markers of quality in the ways people behave—toward us, to others, or alone. In this regard, it pays to be attentive to how individuals perform when they have a chance to show off in semiformal trials of mental and physical skills. Dance and music making provide a special case—a test of how well an individual can keep time, follow a tune, coordinate with others, and so on.

The same goes when we judge a person by the things they create—either for their own use, as gifts, or for public display. We have a critical eye for subtle handiwork, keenness of observation, fine judgment, and good taste, not least as these qualities are expressed in *art*.

Art as advertisement no doubt goes a long way back into the human past. The first paintings were probably decorations applied with red ochre to the skin. Modern examples of body art (figure 5.2) suggest that these would have shown intricate rhyming patterns that, like a bird's plumage, display the bearer's quality.[1]

When, by fifty thousand years ago, humans took to decorating the walls of caves with lifelike pictures of animals, there's every reason to think it was still being done as much for the display of the artist's skill as anything else. Experts on cave art tend to see these paintings as a communal effort and have paid little attention to the possible benefits for the individual artist. Given all we know about human competitiveness, however, it's certain that individuals would have seized the opportunity to show how they excelled.

A notable stylistic feature of European cave art, especially at Chauvet in France, is the occurrence of multiple drawings of

FIGURE 5.2

Men of the "Never Never Land," in Totem Attire, Australia, 1922. In *People of All Nations: Their Life Today and the Story of Their Past,* vol. 1, *Abyssinia to the British Empire,* edited by J. A. Hammerton (Educational Book Company, 1928), 311. Public domain.

FIGURE 5.3
Panel of the Lions, Chauvet Cave, France, c. 32,000 years BP. Replica. Wikimedia Commons.

the same animal species, often superimposed one on another (figure 5.3). If a particular artist was responsible for painting several rhyming variations, then perhaps—like paleolithic Monets—the intention was to capture the essence of the animal.

But could they have been made by different artists, one competing with another to show off his or her skill? How better to prove your worth than to paint over the work of a rival? Think of when Robin Hood, at the sheriff of Nottingham's archery contest, split his rival's arrow down the middle and so gained the hand of Maid Marian.

I have to say the lions' facial expressions look, to me, humanly ambitious.

Forty thousand years later, in 1505, Leonardo da Vinci and Michelangelo di Lodovico Buonarroti Simoni fought a bitter battle for artistic superiority in the Palazzo Vecchio in Florence. They were hired to paint vast battle scenes side by side on the same wall, in direct competition with each other.[2]

We assess potential partners not only for their practical skills but also for markers of quality in their social interactions. We are attracted to "people" people and especially to cooperators. So we look for evidence that individuals are fair-minded and even-handed—that they engage in reciprocity, take turns in conversation, and take turns in life, all examples of rhyme in action.

On top of this, we're attracted to other individuals who *resemble ourselves*—in looks, in smell, in language, and so on—while being different enough to rhyme and be interesting. It means if we mate with them, we'll have compatible genes without being so close as to risk inbreeding; and if we befriend them, we'll have compatible culture and attitudes.

Compatible doesn't necessarily mean symmetric. It can equally mean reciprocal, where one person's strengths make up for another's weaknesses. Jack Sprat and his wife were a good match. On another level I think of the example of my grandparents. My grandfather touchingly wrote a proposal letter to his future wife in 1908: "We might promote a company for the advancement of humanity, in which you and I will be partners, you to act as a reformer of morals and I as a tinker of apparatus."[3]

STRUCTURAL BEAUTY: THE BEAUTY OF CRAFTS

Humans are not only exceptional among animals in the degree to which they rely on each other, but they are also exceptional in their reliance on *things*. Just as we cannot manage without friends, neither can we manage without gear—tools, utensils, weapons, clothing, fences, buildings, and so on.

And we want the best. We want knives that cut cleanly, jugs that pour without spilling, ladders that are stable, bows that shoot straight, knots that don't slip, coats that fit, boats that don't capsize, carts that run smoothly, and shelters that withstand the wind. These requirements are critically important. The choice of an axe may not be as crucial to a man as the choice of a wife is, but his life may depend on it all the same.

Sometimes we find ourselves choosing among ready-mades, but often we have to make the things by ourselves. For most of human history, our ancestors have had to be accomplished do-it-yourselfers. It's been up to us as individuals to knap flints, light fires, mold clay, sew cloth, plait ropes, dig trenches, build walls, and so on. We probably learned how to go about these jobs by watching other people do them, but their completion always depended on our having an eye for what works, what's stable, what's going to endure. As we start on a project, we must know what it is we're aiming to achieve. We have to be able to imagine the shape of the finished axe in the mother flint and to know when to stop chipping.

So what are the surface features that guide us to recognizing good functional design in things? As it happens, they are much the same as we use for recognizing a well-designed human being. Symmetry, balance, and rhyme will be key considerations—a spear tapered to a point, a ladder with evenly spaced rungs, a boat with nicely graded ribs, a wheel perfectly rounded, a matching pair of shoes, a conical wigwam.

And there's one feature that will have proved singularly important in the evolution of technology. At some point, our ancestors realized how things could *lock together* to provide a larger whole with emergent features. They saw how to string a bow, to fit a haft to a spear (figure 5.4), to interlace stones to produce a sturdy wall. They had begun to appreciate the

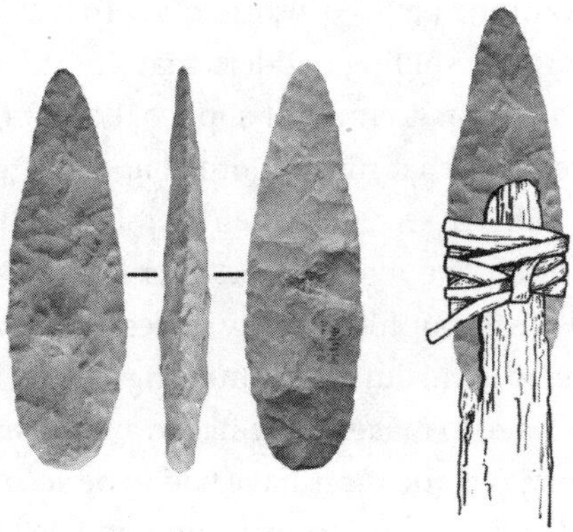

FIGURE 5.4
Stone spear and haft, Congo basin, 0.3 million years BP. From Nicholas Taylor, "Hypothetical Hafting of a Lupemban Lanceolate Point Excavated from Kalambo Falls, Zambia. Haft Illustration after Barham 2001," in "The Origins of Hunting and Gathering in the Congo Basin: A Perspective on the Middle Stone Age Lupemban Industry," *Hunter Gatherer Research* (2011): 1, art. 6, fig. 3. By kind permission of N. Taylor and L. Barham.

practical possibilities of reciprocal rhyme as a principle of engineering.

Figure 5.5 shows the engineer John Smeaton's design for the Eddystone lighthouse, which he modeled on the trunk and boughs of an oak tree. Note the interlocking pattern of the stonework. Although such dovetailing is a regular feature of plant and animal internal anatomy, it's only humans who have seen how to build external structures on the same principle.

I remarked above, in relation to personal beauty, how the combination of one person with another person can create an entity whose capabilities exceed the sum of its parts. The same can happen with ideas: One thought can become the key to its inverse (or the universe).

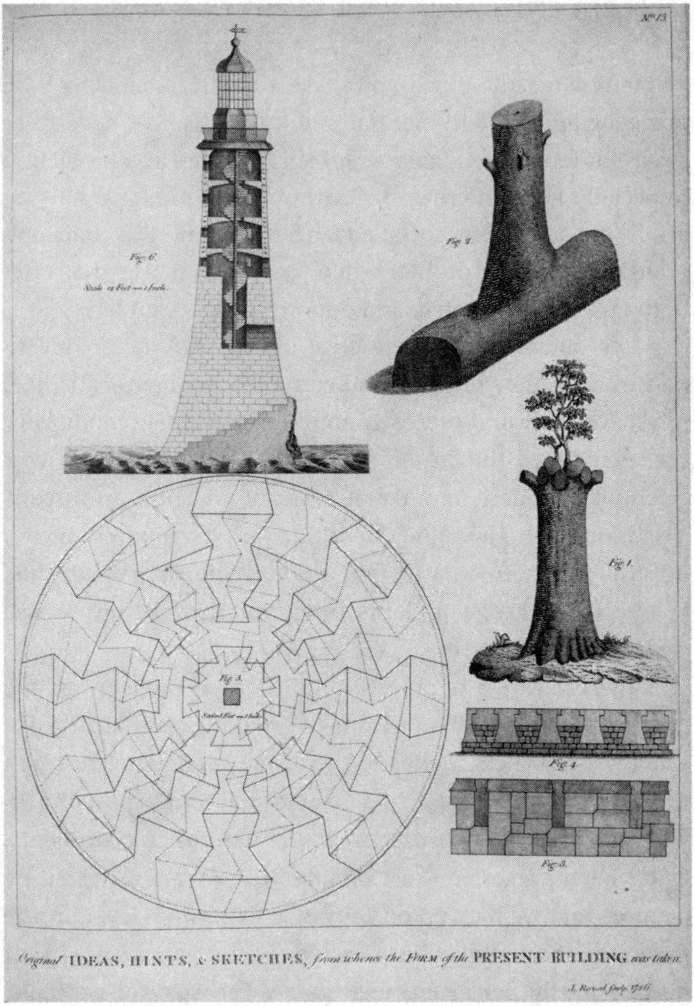

FIGURE 5.5

Preliminary sketches for John Smeaton's Eddystone lighthouse, c. 1756. From John Smeaton, *A Narrative of the Building and a Description of the Construction of the Edystone Lighthouse with Stone* (Printed for the author by H. Hughs, c. 1791), plate 13. In the public domain.

ENVIRONMENTAL BEAUTY: THE BEAUTY OF PLACES

Humans can settle down and make a life in remarkably various geographical and cultural environments. We have basic needs for food, water, companionship, shelter, and protection (especially from the threats posed by other humans); but we also crave adventure, social advancement, and the chance to branch out. So we do best when we live in places that offer both guarantees of safety and opportunities for growth.

Since our ancestors were creatures of the African savannah who lived by hunting and gathering, we are preadapted, physiologically and mentally, to living in similar conditions. It's been called the *biophilia hypothesis*—the suggestion that in choosing where to make our homes, we show an instinctive liking for the "greenness" (in all its modern meanings) of nature in balance, the rhymes and rhythms of life. Where a wide range of plants and animals are happy, so will we be.[4]

This is hardly a hypothesis and more a statement of the obvious—not so different from the hypothesis that fish like water. Nonetheless, it has led to some interesting research that asks what sensory cues people may be responding to when they feel drawn to sustainable natural environments. It has been suggested, for example, that we are attracted by features that we pick up on only at a subliminal level, in the same way that we may be attracted to a sexual partner by an unconsciously perceived pheromone. Perhaps, for example, we have an eye for the "fractal structure" of the landscape (the rhyming patterns repeated on several different scales) that is a characteristic of rich ecosystems such as forests and other green spaces.[5]

This fits well with modern concerns. But an overly reverential attitude toward biophilia has meant that environmental psychologists have tended to neglect other choices people make. While people may profess to prefer living in the countryside, the fact is they frequently vote with their feet to live in towns.[6] And it's not just people. Other animals that we might expect because of their evolutionary history to be no less biophilic than humans—foxes, pigeons, monkeys, rats—are ready enough to adopt an urban lifestyle when they have the chance.

In the case of these animals, the probable reason is that they gain better access to food and possibly freedom from predators (the rats of the New York subway don't have to worry about owls). With humans, however, there's more to it. They crave social goods.

Early humans who lived in the wild as hunters and gatherers were able to do so only as members of close-knit tribal groups committed to mutual aid and cooperation. As the groups grew larger and more settled, they began to take on additional communal responsibilities—to control resources such as food and water, to enforce fair dealing, to provide orderly administration, and, most important, to protect the community from external enemies. Since our ancestors depended for so long on this social landscape, it makes sense that today, in addition to our liking for wild spaces, we also gravitate to places that show evidence of institutional stability where as individuals we can expect to be accommodated and protected.

What forms will this take? How do communities reassure their members that their interests are being and will continue to be looked after? One way is by laying on activities that directly encourage group cohesion—public rituals, dances,

FIGURE 5.6
Stonehenge, c. 4,500 years BP. Photo by Steve Lee. © FDR-Promotions. By kind permission.

feasts, and so on. A second way is by creating public works of art.

Civic art down the ages celebrates orderly governance (figures 5.6 and 5.7). Stones are made to stand upright in circles. Rough surfaces are carpeted with interlocking floral patterns. Trees are planted in straight avenues. Fountains gush water in elegant cascades. Church bells ring the changes. Bands march in strict formation. Choirs sing in harmony.

Architectural monuments everywhere—from castles to temples to railway stations, with their bold rhymes in stone and steel—are designed to show that these are places where law and order prevail and are here to stay. That is the message of the Moscow Metro, the Taj Mahal, Westminster Abbey, the Colosseum, and the Parthenon. Further back are the Egyptian pyramids and Stonehenge. More ancient still, at Gobekli Tepe—the eight thousand-year-old site in Turkey dominated by temples—it's been suggested that people from far afield

FIGURE 5.7
Darlington train station, 1887. Photo by Mike Butt. Wikipedia. Creative Commons. Attribution-Share Alike 2.0 generic license.

gathered at annual festivals to get a booster shot of "citizenship" (even though they did not yet live in cities).[7]

I would guess that people who visited the painted caves of Lascaux and Chauvet in their heyday also felt community pride. It is usually assumed that the purpose of the paintings was to celebrate and even worship the animals that were depicted. Yet when the art historian Ernst Gombrich first saw photos of the Chauvet paintings, his astonished response was "*Man* is a great miracle." For him, the paintings were primarily about the greatness of being human.[8]

Putting aside my suggestion that the caves were a display case for individual artists to show off their skills, I wonder whether visitors arriving generations later read them, just as Gombrich did, as a testament to the excellence of their tribe:

"Look at what our ancestors have done! See how they've made wild animals—the very lions and horses—dance to their tune!" It may be relevant that footprints found in the Chauvet cave appear to be those of an eight-year-old boy. If you want to shape community spirit, get in early. As the Jesuits taught: "Give me the child until the age of seven, and I will give you the man."

6 HE'S GOT THE WHOLE WORLD IN HIS HANDS

Rhyming environments give us a feeling of security. Of love. Let me dwell on this, even if it's a bit of a diversion. For it means that perceived beauty can impact human welfare in surprising ways.

Personal safety is never far from people's minds. John Dos Passos in his novel *The Big Money* summed up the human predicament as he saw it: "Tell us, doctors of philosophy, what are the needs of a man. At least a man needs to be notjailed notafraid nothungry notcold, not without love, not a worker for a power he has never seen that cares nothing for the uses and needs of a man or a woman or a child."[1] Needs are defined by what is wanting. What do we want? A safe haven. When do we want it? Now.

Dos Passos may have been writing about life in the context of twentieth-century capitalism. But his diagnosis fits the more distant human past as well. For much of the last million years, our ancestors have led lives riddled with anxiety—short of food, liable to recurrent illness, beset by sudden changes in the climate, at risk of predation, and under threat of physical and psychological aggression from other humans. They have suffered more than any nonhuman animal can because of their capacity for imagination and mental time travel. Only humans are death-aware. Only humans have a conscious need nottobeextinguished.

It's to be expected, then, that we should have inherited a chronic tendency to fear the worst. And indeed, physiological measures show that our brains and glands remain in a continuing state of stress unless and until we see positive signs of safety. In a paper setting out a generalized unsafety theory of stress, Jos Brosschot and his colleagues wrote that

> The stress response is always "on," and it stays on as long as there is no obvious safety. When safety is perceived, the stress response is inhibited. Importantly, to be "on" it does not need a stressor at all: it either remains activated as long as no safety is perceived or is disinhibited when safety disappears. It is a "default" response, meaning that it is a preselected condition to which the system (the organism) falls back when there is no other input, i.e. no relevant information, which for the stress response is information regarding safety. The default here is a state of generalized unsafety in which the stress response stays on.[2]

In work of my own relating to how humans and other animals have evolved to regulate their bodily and mental health, I have argued that we possess what I've called a natural health management system with a "central health governor" in the brain whose primary role is to manage risk (figure 6.1).[3] The governor constantly monitors the environment to see what hazards or opportunities are coming down the road. It then adjusts our physiology and behavior according to the forecast—relaxing only when things appear to be set fair, battening down the hatches when they look rough.

The default strategy is highly conservative. It's designed so that, in the absence of clear evidence that we're in a secure

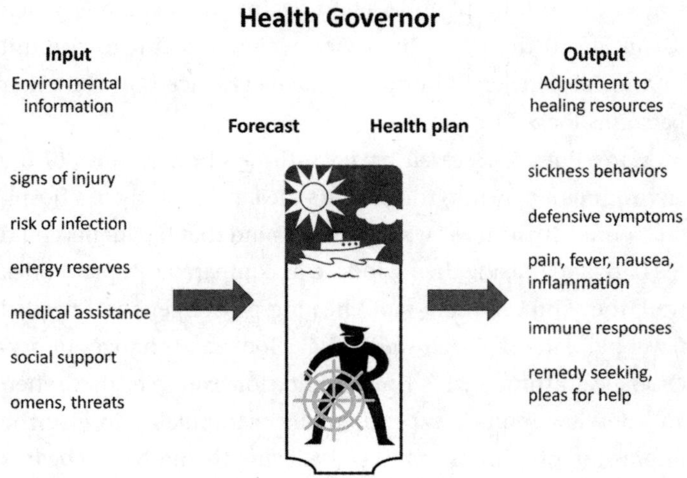

FIGURE 6.1
The central health governor. From Nicholas Humphrey and John Skoyles, "The Evolutionary Psychology of Healing: A Human Success Story," *Current Biology* 22 (2012): R1–R4.

place materially and socially, we tread warily and save rather than spend. For example, we will not wind down a defensive response to injury, such as feeling pain, until we are assured that we are not going to be exposed to further trauma. We will not splash out on an immune response to an infection, such as a cold virus, until we have evidence that we can replenish our immune reserves by access to appropriate food. When it comes to social relationships, we will continue to be suspicious of another person's motives until we have positive proof of their trustworthiness.

That's why a young boy will feel the pain of a stinging nettle until his mother takes him in her arms and kisses the sting better. That's why our immune system tends to hold back on its response to a cold virus in winter, when food might be scarce, but throws its full weight against it in summer when it can afford the risk. That's why we're reluctant to commit to a social partnership until we have evidence that the other person is locked in.

Many lines of research have confirmed how features of the environment play into this. There's the famous study of a hospital "room with a view," where it was found that if patients could see parkland outside their window, as compared to a plain brick wall, they showed more rapid healing postsurgery and needed fewer painkillers.[4] Other studies have looked at changes in psychological attitudes. It's been found, for example, that when an interview room is experimentally manipulated to give the impression of tidiness, subjects (believing themselves to be in a safer environment) are more likely to donate to charity.[5] Similarly, when they are given the chance to play an online trust game with someone whose home they are shown in a photograph, they are more likely to cooperate with a partner who appears to live in a neat home rather than a run-down one.[6]

The safety level need not be registered consciously. Brosschot and his colleagues draw attention to how information about the physical and social environment, perceived at an unconscious level, can elicit or suppress the stress response: "[In the case of] loneliness, low social status, prenatal or early life adversity, lack of a natural environment . . . the default stress response may be chronically disinhibited due to *unconsciously perceived* generalized unsafety."

A remarkable demonstration of how unconscious influence can be brought to bear came in an experiment by Haruaki Fukuda and his colleagues.[7] They tested whether people playing the prisoner's dilemma game against an online partner—a game where they have to choose whether to cooperate or defect—would be influenced by a subtle cue to cooperation present in the room. The participants were seated at a desk and played the game on a laptop computer in front of them. Meanwhile, to the side of the desk was another laptop on whose screen a simple animation was playing over and over, apparently as a screensaver. The animation showed a green ball and a red ball interacting in either a "helpful" or a "hindering" way. In the "help mode," the green ball nudged the red in the direction the red ball was traveling, while in the "hinder mode," the green ball got in the way of the red and knocked it backward.

The participants had no reason to attend to this second computer, and none remarked on it. Nevertheless, when it came to playing the game, those who were exposed to the helpful animation collaborated more than 70 percent of the time, while those exposed to the hindering animation did so less than 30 percent.

The overall conclusion is strong: While people may indeed generally expect the worst, they are ready to welcome evidence that this stance is unwarranted, that things are okay. This may often come down to the presence of strong hints of order, balance, and fairness in the environment.

The studies where expectations were artificially manipulated tell us something else of great significance. The participants in these studies were being *misled*: The "safety or unsafety" signals were merely make-believe. And it isn't only humans who can fall for such "spurious evidence." An experiment with Siberian hamsters manipulated their expectations about the season of the year by keeping them on an artificial day and night light cycle that corresponded either to summer or winter. Both groups of hamsters were then injected with bacteria that made them ill. In the event, the hamsters who were tricked into "thinking" it was winter held back on their immune response, but those who "thought" it was summer threw everything they had against the infection, developed a high fever and anorexia, and eliminated the bacteria.[8]

You might think that the fact that the health governor can be duped into relaxing its guard by signals that have no genuine bearing on the subject's prospects points to a weakness in the design of the natural health management system. And, yes, potentially it does so. Yet remarkably enough, it's a weakness that can turn out to be a blessing. Its upside is the possibility of the *placebo effect*.

It's well known to doctors that false promises of medical treatment can induce patients to heal themselves before the external circumstances warrant it. For example, they drop precautionary defenses such as pain or release precious immune resources even though the safety level hasn't really changed. Not so well known is the placebo effect in social psychology, where spurious evidence of social order can bring about positive changes in people's personalities and attitudes. The study I quoted above, where "tidiness" was experimentally manipulated, took advantage of this loophole.

Here's the implication for our discussion. If mere hints of safety can have these effects in an experiment, then so too in real life could "community architecture" of the kind I lauded in the previous chapter. Who's to say that Stonehenge itself didn't act as a placebo? In fact, there's reason to think that historically Stonehenge may have done this. In 1215, the English poet Layamon, inspired by earlier folkloric accounts, described how Stonehenge was once a place that sick people visited for miracle cures:[9]

> The stones are great
> And magic power they have
> Men that are sick

Fare to that stone
And they wash that stone
And with that water bathe away their sickness

* * *

We should note that the placebo effect comes with risks. We usually think of self-healing as an unmitigated boon. But it cannot always be a good use of our resources to respond to the promise of relief before the external circumstances warrant it. If the safety signals are false, it means we are being induced to self-heal before it is wise to do so. When we respond to quack doctors by squandering precious immune resources or to quack blandishments from propagandists by letting down our guard, we may be left dangerously exposed.

That's true. But having made the point, I'm immediately going to qualify it. It may be a mistake to assume that the background levels of risk have remained unchanged down the years. Suppose the reality is that the world in which we live today is considerably less precarious than it was when the settings of the health governor were put in place by natural selection. Then these ancient settings will now be *overcautious*. In that case, if we respond to spurious safety signals by liberating healing resources kept in reserve, this may be what's needed (or what the doctor ordered) to induce us to act in our own best interests.

With this possibility in mind—that in the modern world we may depend on placebos to encourage us to escape from our out-of-date protective shells—I want to suggest a significant role for a special category of environmental beauty.

So far, I've discussed signals emanating from parts of our social and geographical environment that we might reasonably expect to be relevant to assessing what the future holds for us. In these contexts, as a general rule, rhyme can be taken to be a sign of safety. But there are other features of our surroundings whose rhymes have no bearing whatsoever on our human prospects—distant mountains, the aurora borealis, waves breaking on the beach, the design of a seashell, the song of a skylark, the chestnut fan.

"Life is sweet, brother," Jasper, the gypsy, assures George Borrow in the autobiographical novel *Lavengro*: "There's night and day, brother, both sweet things; sun, moon, and stars, brother, all sweet things. . . . There's the wind on the heath, brother; if I could only feel that, I would gladly live for ever."[10] Sweet and beautiful things. But they don't have much to do with human welfare.

Unless, that is, we choose to see it that way. What if we *imagine* that these natural phenomena too are safety signals or even that they are evidence of somebody trying to tell us something? "Does anyone feel the same kind of emotion," Clive Bell asked, "for a butterfly or a flower"—or, let's say, a rainbow—"that he feels for a cathedral or a picture?"[11] Bell assumed the answer must be no, because we don't feel emotionally connected to the *artists* who made them. But what if we were to believe that these works of nature have been created and put there for a purpose?

I say "what if," but in reality, I think there's no *if* about it. From all we know about evolved human psychology, we know that whenever people see evidence of design in either the man-made or the natural world, their "intentionality detectors" are activated. Their default assumption is that some form of creative intelligence lies behind it.

Teleological reasoning—the assumption that everything happens for a purpose—is deeply embedded in the human psyche. It's especially strong in children, who have been described as born creationists. But it never deserts us. Research to test people's intuitions that "the world and features in it were purposefully made by some being" has been run with subjects ranging from elite scientists to religious believers and avowed atheists, in America and China, and the findings are everywhere the same: Creationist thinking appears to be the default mode.[12]

William Paley, in the famous thought experiment I cited earlier, asked readers to imagine they were walking on a heath and were to stumble across a pocket watch lying in the grass. They would conclude that the watch was the work of a watchmaker. So when we stumble across a rainbow arching across the field, the same reasoning is sure to apply. Our first thought will be—and perhaps should be—that it's the work of a rainbow maker. Even if we don't make the reasoning explicit, a voice will whisper it in our ear.

A rainbow maker has to be *some maker.* Let's imagine we received a rainbow as a gift from a suitor. We'd have every reason to see it as a demonstration of their skill, intelligence, and good taste. When Giotto was asked by Pope Benedict XI to prove his skill as a painter, he drew a perfect circle freehand. The artist of the rainbow has gone one better and colored it in.

Imagine we found ourselves in a human habitation decorated with man-made rainbows. We'd surely assume these were the public symbols of a peaceful and well-governed community. Remember, in the story in Genesis, that Yahweh created a flood to wash away humanity's corruption and then put the rainbow in the sky as the sign of his promise that he would never again bring on such destruction: "Whenever the rainbow appears in the clouds, I will see it and remember the everlasting covenant between God and all living creatures of every kind on the earth."[13] In modern times, think of the use made by the LGBT community of the rainbow symbol to flag a safe haven.

The world over, people believe that natural phenomena channel supernatural beings. In the Christian tradition, God announces his love for us through the works of his creation. If the beauties of nature are a gift, they are gift from God. If they are posted as a reminder to live within the laws, they are God's laws. In the words of the African American spiritual, he holds the whole world in his hands:

> He's got the ends of the earth in his hands,
> He's got the crashing of the waves in his hands,
> He's got the high mighty mountains in his hands,
> He's got the whole world in his hands!
>
> He's got the dawning of the morning in his hands,
> He's got the last rays of sunshine in his hands,
> He's got the sweet falling rain in his hands,
> He's got the whole world in his hands!

Here's my scientific point: This way of thinking cannot be neutral. In fact, I would expect that, because of the placebo effect, it is likely to have major practical consequences for human psychology and physiology. When people are regularly exposed to the messages of good governance implicit in the beauties of nature, then—however unjustified by the reality—this may go a long way to countering their innate pessimism and so allow them *to dare to thrive*.

* * *

I'll make a more specific suggestion. In many religious traditions, God is seen not only as a creator and benign administrator but also as a father figure. And for human health, this could be of considerable significance. It's an axiom of sociobiology that a person's parentage is one of the major determinants of how their lives play out. We should expect this to be something the health governor takes into account when forecasting risks.

Numerous studies have, in fact, shown that children of dominant and successful parents—alpha males and females—are most likely to take the high road in life, adapting their physiology and personality so as to make the wise and healthy choices that potentially lead to better outcomes. By contrast, children who grow up with poor or absent parents are likely to aim much lower. The evolutionary basis for this has been well explained. Essentially, the more that children have invested in them by their parents, the less pressure there will be for them to go after short-term gains, and so the more scope they will have to plan for the long term.

This leads to a prediction. For individuals who have had inadequate or absent parents (and there have been historical periods when this is likely to have been most of them), the belief that they nonetheless have God as a father—the alpha male if there ever was one—would have brought about a major shift in the health governor's forecasts. Thus, in the hope that their lives will, after all, turn out better than they might have otherwise expected, they will take the longer view and set higher goals for themselves.

This prediction has, so far as I know, never been tested directly. But what is well established is that, in general, religious beliefs have positive effects on physical and mental health and are associated with greater within-group moral attitudes. If, as we've seen, people's belief in God is consequent on their recognizing harmony and order in nature, we have here an additional explanation for why humans would have benefited from living in the presence of rhyme.

7 THE TANGLED BANK

I hope you'll be thinking that this all seems pretty convincing. In answer to the question "How does rhyme relate to human welfare?," we've come up with more than a few useful rules of thumb:

- Make friends with—and make love to—rhyming people.
- Furnish your home base with rhyming artefacts.
- Keep company with rhyming plants and animals.
- Settle in a place that's full of rhyming public art.
- Worship the creator for the rhymes of nature.

If we follow these rules, many of our biological and social needs are likely to be met. And if the attraction to rhyme "accidentally" spills over to other cases where the benefits are marginal or nonexistent (nursery rhymes, say, or conceptual art), that's presumably not going to matter.

Perhaps this is enough to explain why humans have evolved to be attracted to rhyme across the board.

Consider the following imaginary scenario. Humans of the past discovered that yellow-haired people made good mates, yellow buildings stood up to the wind, and yellow brick roads got them to safety. Over time, this led to the evolution of a universal yellow detector in the human brain and a behavioral attraction to yellow things in general. There were major benefits to be had from being attracted to yellow-haired people, yellow buildings, and yellow roads and, let's assume, no great costs to being attracted to yellow flowers, yellow gemstones, and yellow submarines.

Now substitute "rhyming" for "yellow," and we have arrived at an explanation of the evolution of a universal rhyme detector.

This explanation sounds plausible. It jibes with the ideas of evolutionary psychologists. And I'm pretty sure it's right in parts. But I am still only half—actually, less than half—persuaded by it. For I believe a much neater explanation is waiting in the wings.

Let me return to that guiding statement by Thomas Reid. The task before us, he said, is to "discover some real excellence in the [beautiful] object, or, at least, some valuable purpose that is served by the effect which it produces upon us." Our discussion so far has focused only on the first part—excellence *in the object*, which we can exploit in practical ways by remaining in its presence.

But we should note that Reid raised a second possibility—that there is some valuable purpose served by *the effect of the object on us*. He didn't explain quite what he meant. But I guess he was alluding to the subjective experience of beauty and the lasting impression it leaves on our minds. If *that's* where the valuable purpose lies, then we ought to be asking a different question—not "How do people benefit directly from the existence of rhyming objects?" but "How do they benefit from the experience of rhyme as a mental activity?"

This harks straight back to Immanuel Kant. I quoted him in chapter 1: "When the question is whether a thing be beautiful, we do not want to know whether anything depends or can depend, for us or for anyone else, on the existence of the object, but only how we estimate it in pure contemplation."

I expressed doubts, initially, about where this could take us. Presumably, the love of beauty can contribute to biological survival only by affecting how we, as individuals, relate to the outside world. If "pure contemplation" were to mean some kind of disconnected reverie in which we have no personal interest in the existence of the objects at the center of it, the benefits to us could be only minimal. But there's a different way of reading it. What if we take pure contemplation to mean mindful engagement with the things as such—the things in their own right, not in ours?

This would be to contemplate things in the way Charles Darwin did, as an inquiry into their essential form.

At the close of *The Origin of Species*, Darwin wrote:

> It is interesting to contemplate an entangled bank, clothed with many plants of many kinds, with birds singing on the bushes, with various insects flitting about, and with worms crawling through the damp earth, and to reflect that these elaborately constructed forms, so different from each other, and dependent on each other in so complex a manner, have all been produced by laws acting around us. . . . There is grandeur in this view of life, with its several powers, having been originally breathed into a few forms or into one; and that, whilst this planet has gone cycling on according to the fixed law of gravity, from so simple a beginning endless forms most beautiful and most wonderful have been, and are being, evolved.[1]

Darwin saw the bank not as a practical resource but as a tangle of meaning (figure 7.1). As a challenge to our intellectual

FIGURE 7.1
J. Ann Aldridge, *The Tangled Bank*, 2025. © J. Ann Eldridge. By kind permission of the artist.

powers of discernment. As an invitation to construct a story about how things connect to each other and to their own past.

With this example, I want to turn our discussion onto a different path. I don't doubt that benefits of the kind we've identified in the preceding chapters could be helping to underpin and maintain the human love of rhyme. But I want to move to an alternative idea about its primary function—that through attending to rhymes in the environment, wherever we may find them, we enlarge our cognitive horizons.

8 THE JOY OF ORDER

We humans, like all free-living animals, rely on having a "world model" in our heads—a mental representation of what the world contains and how it works. This model reduces the thought load on us and allows rapid and efficient extrapolation from one set of circumstances to another. It helps us anticipate what is likely to happen next and plan our own behavior accordingly.

It's our good fortune (I'll say more about this later) that the world we live in is in fact quite a regular place. There are *rules* that govern how events play out in time: Water flows downhill, night follows day, the early bird catches the worm, one good turn begets another, and so on. We have to get to know these rules and incorporate them into our model. Even more basic, the world contains *kinds of things* that can be relied on to have similar properties from one occasion to the next—dogs, chairs, trees, biscuits, numbers, and so on. We must be able to recognize these kinds and the ways they typically behave.

Luckily, it doesn't all have to be learned. The laws of nature—and even those of society—don't change much. Moreover, the kinds of things we encounter have to some extent always been the same. This means that parts of the world model may already have been filled in by evolution and have become embedded as innate ideas. Nonetheless—especially for creatures such as humans, who are born into in diverse and unstable environments—much of the detailed information must still be acquired through personal experience. Every human infant must start by discovering just what kinds of things exist in *their* world.

The task of classifying things is made much easier (I might say it's made possible) by the fact that here on earth, most of the things that interest us do have family relationships. When we group things into classes defined by shared properties, the classes will often form a nested hierarchy. This is as true of the physical world as it is of the biological world and the social world. Raindrops combine to form streams, streams give rise to rivers, rivers form seas. Sarah is my sister, my sister is a child of my parents, my parents and all my kin belong to my tribe. Apples are fruit, fruits grow on trees, trees grow in orchards, and so on.

Classification remains an art. Each of us has to make choices in line with our particular interests and exposure to events. However, there is, as it happens, a simple heuristic we can use to guide us. Remember how I defined rhyme in chapter 3: "Two entities, A and B, rhyme when we recognize that, while they differ, they belong together. . . . Typically, this comes about when A and B have some 'essential' property in common, while they differ in respect of some 'contingent property.'" In the cognitive act of noticing the rhyme between any two things, we are creating a class—trying it on for size, as it were.

* * *

Imagine yourself as an infant setting out to discover the kinds of things the world—*your* world—contains. You have an innate motivation to develop a system of categories, but the actual system you arrive at must be largely based on your own experience. Your task is similar to the one faced by a zoological taxonomist who sets out to classify the animals in their locality. How should you—how should the zoologist—proceed?

For the sake of argument, I'll make this very simple. I suggest you have to work through the following stages:

1. You make a preliminary reconnaissance and come up with certain hunches about what sorts of things are out there and what their distinguishing criteria are.
2. You seek further evidence to test the "validity" of these initial guesses and at the same time to acquaint yourself with the diversity that may exist within each class.
3. To the extent that your criteria prove successful, you adopt them as permanent guidelines for future classification, while to the extent that they fail, you abandon or revise them.

Successful criteria will be those that yield a system of classification that is, at once, *unambiguous* (an object either belongs to a class or it doesn't), *exhaustive* (every object belongs to some class or another), and *useful* (objects in the same class may be treated for some practical purpose as the same).

As a zoologist, you might start, for example, with a classification of animals that divides them into vertebrates and invertebrates. This would meet all three requirements. But a division into meat eaters and plant eaters would fail to be unambiguous since some eat both. A division into swimming animals and flying animals would fail to be exhaustive since some animals neither swim nor fly. A division into animals that live in zoos and animals that live in the wild would fail to be useful since there is no purpose (for a zoologist) in treating the members of either of these classes as the same.

Suppose you have a particular interest in warm-blooded vertebrates. In making a preliminary survey, you meet a cat, a dog, and a hen, and you notice that the cat and the dog are covered with hair while the hen is covered with feathers. Taking these to be distinctive criteria, you set up two putative classes that you label "mammals" and "birds."

Your next step is to look for further examples to test how well this division works. Suppose the next animals you meet are a horse and then a rabbit. Applying your criteria, you discover that these animals fit neatly into the category of mammals. Then perhaps you meet a sparrow, then a mouse, and then a parrot, and you are pleased to find that while the mouse is clearly a mammal, the sparrow and the parrot fit the definition of a bird. Looking further, you meet another cat, but on this occasion, you pay it little attention since seeing additional cats tells you nothing new. Later on, you meet an octopus. But since this is not a warm-blooded vertebrate, it can provide no evidence either way, and again you pay it no attention.

Certain principles of how to gather evidence are beginning to emerge. You need to establish that your criteria enable you to label any of the animals you are interested in as either a mammal or a bird. Accordingly, you look for two sets of examples—animals that have either hair in common (but not feathers) or feathers in common (but not hair). But you have nothing to learn from seeing repetitive examples of the same kind of animal or in seeing an animal that is so different as to lie outside the scope of your inquiry. In short, you look for examples of rhyming animals.

Pursuing the metaphor of a "taxonomic poem":

> Cats rhyme with dogs, horses, and other hairy animals.
> Hens rhyme with parrots, sparrows, and other feathery animals.
> Octopuses do not rhyme with either.

So far so good. As a zoologist, you may decide to stop there. But if you are an ordinary human infant, you'll probably want to take things further. You'll want to be able to recognize not just cats as mammals but also cats as distinct from dogs. You'll want to recognize different breeds of cat (Siamese cats as distinct from Persian cats), your cat Moggie as distinct from your neighbor's cat Pansy, and Moggie as seen at different times and from different perspectives.

None of this may be relevant to a zoologist, but it's highly relevant to you. So, for you, there will be rhymes to be discovered *between* cats and *within* a single cat:

> Siamese cats rhyme with Persian cats.
> Moggie one day rhymes with Moggie another day.
> Moggie seen from the front rhymes with Moggie seen from the back.

How deep you take the classification will depend on how deep you need to go to serve your interests. As we'll see shortly, this can change—and so will your attention to rhyme.

* * *

For the same reason that this is an effective way for you to discover how things are connected and divided, it will presumably be an effective way for someone to *teach* it to you. A good teacher will shortcut the exploration and present you with rhyming examples side by side so that the similarities and differences stand out. "Teaching through rhyme" is indeed a tried and trusted method in many real-life educational settings, like museums, sample books, and grammars.

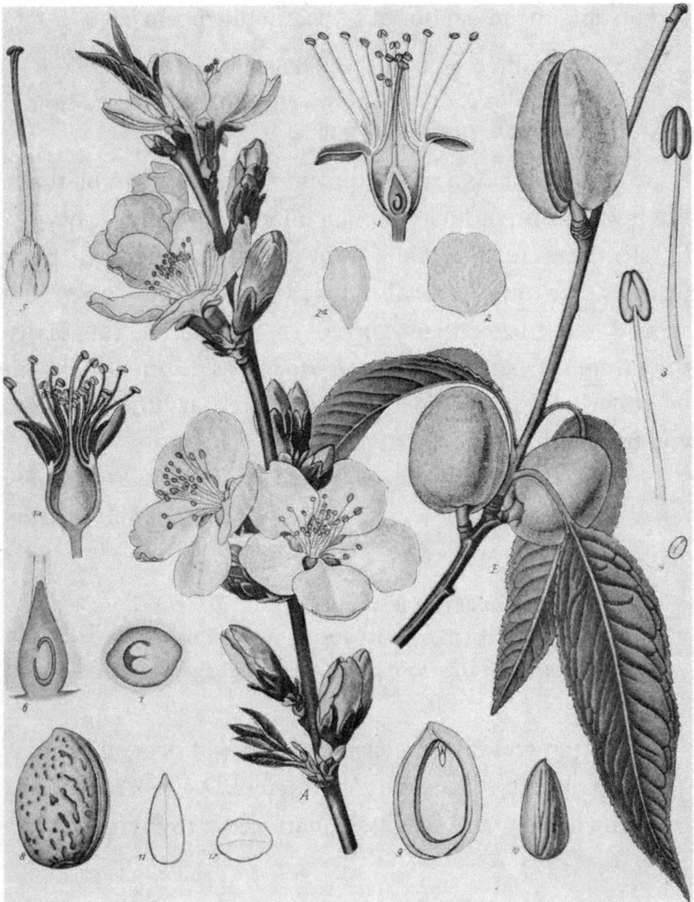

FIGURE 8.1
Almond tree flowers, fruits, and nuts. From Hermann Adolph Köhler, *Köhler's Medizinal-Pflanzen*, ed. Gustav Pabst (Franz Eugen Köhler, 1900). American Museum of Natural History Library, https://picryl.com/media/birds-and-nature-1900-14746875061-bcac3a. In public domain.

Perhaps the most obvious and pertinent application is in zoological and botanical field guides. There is a long tradition of botanical illustration where a single plate shows the same kind of plant from different perspectives and in different stages of development—in bud, in flower, in seed, in cross section, and so on. The purpose is to help students recognize not only how one species of plant differs from another but also how an individual plant may appear at different times. Figure 8.1 shows a typical example—a composite drawing of an almond tree.

Would it be going too far to say that this botanical drawing employs a similar strategy for revealing *essential form* that Chopin does in his sonatas or Monet in his views of Rouen cathedral? I'll say it anyway: A picture like this resembles a musical composition. Look at it again.

For balance, however, I'll offer a less highbrow analogy. The botanical drawing employs a teaching strategy quite similar to that now used to train artificial intelligence to recognize specific kinds of object. For example, the training program for "teledermatology" feeds an artificial neural network hundreds of examples of photos of cancerous lesions at different stages and on different types of skin so that the artificial intelligence (AI) can compare and contrast the data until it picks out the rhyming patterns (figure 8.2).[1]

True, the "training set" that is fed to the AI is generally much messier than the training set presented in a botanical illustration. In the latter, the illustrator preselects nice examples and arranges them in a way that helps viewers make pertinent comparisons. But the principle of teaching through rhyme is the same.

Nonethless I don't mean to put much weight on teaching. For human infants, teaching by an outsider is usually of

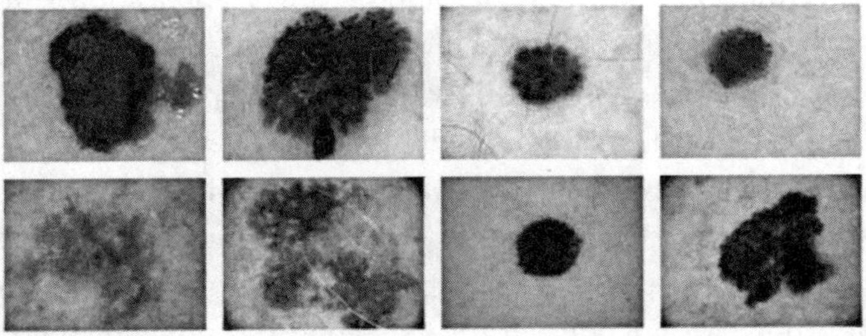

FIGURE 8.2
Melanoma skin lesions. From Sara Nasiri, Julien Helsper, Matthias Jung, and Madjid Fathi, "DePicT Melanoma Deep-CLASS: A Deep Convolutional Neural Networks Approach to Classify Skin Lesion Images," *BMC Bioinformatics* 21 (suppl. 2), no. 84 (March 11, 2020): fig. 7.

secondary importance. In the wilderness of things that each of us is born to, we must be both learner and teacher rolled into one.

This is the central idea that I'm going to promote from here on. Even if rhyme were to have nothing else to recommend it—even without any material benefits from interacting with rhyming objects—cognitive model building could provide a sufficient explanation for why we seek it out. By taking pleasure in the pure experience of rhyme, *we provide the training sets for our own minds*.

But there are interesting side issues. First, I want to say something about poetry.

9 "THE BEFORE UNAPPREHENDED RELATIONS OF THINGS"

The idea we've come to is that rhyme—whether it's between clouds, chemical elements, almonds, or skin lesions—can reveal actual resemblances between things that are, as it were, waiting to be uncovered: groupings that correspond to underlying facts of nature. That's how attending to rhyme helps us bring our mental models into correspondence with *reality*. But perhaps that's only the beginning.

For most people, the paradigm example of rhyme is probably the sounds of spoken verse. I've used the metaphor of a taxonomic "poem." But poetry is an art form where objectivity is not necessarily part of the bargain. W. H. Auden said of poetry: "What makes it difficult for a poet not to tell lies is that in poetry, all facts and all beliefs cease to be true or false and become interesting possibilities."[1]

Rhymes cannot exactly lie, but they can certainly mislead. As we saw in the case of coincidences (featured in the gallery in chapter 4), they can hint at significant similarities between things when all there is to it is the fact that *to us they rhyme*. Cats and mats, for example, happen to have names that sound the same to us, but they have no other essential property in common. A weasel and a weasel-shaped cloud may look the same to us, but that's as far as the resemblance goes. When Eminem rhymed "Munchausen's Syndrome" and "public housin' systems," he was bringing together concepts that are totally unrelated—or, at any rate, unrelated until then.

Fortuitous or accidental rhymes may or may not spike our interest. Most of them are stillborn and go nowhere. However, every now and again the rhyme can lead to a union of ideas that is genuinely fruitful. This is where poetic invention takes off. The formal structure of the poem forces poets to play around semirandomly with the *sounds of words* until they hit on a rhyme that shows previously unrelated things in a new light.

The mathematician Stanislas Ulam described how as a boy he discovered this route to creativity: "I felt that the role of rhyme in poetry was to compel one to find the unobvious because of the necessity of finding a word which rhymes. This forces novel associations and almost guarantees deviations from routine chains or trains of thought. It becomes paradoxically a sort of automatic mechanism of originality."[2]

As John Hollander, himself a poet, has put it:

And verse can be a charm to conjure up
A ghost of meaning in an empty cup . . .
. . .
In a mere accident of common sound
A hidden jewel of meaning, hard and bright,
Bred by the pressure of the ear's delight.[3]

But the poetry doesn't have to be written by a poet or painted by a painter. The accidental rhymes and rhythms of the natural world can equally act as a factory of originality, where ideas that were strangers to each other are brought together in our minds—and, as evolutionary theorist Matt Ridley has put it, end up having sex.[4]

The same can occur with ordinary spoken language. Because the sounds of most words are unrelated to their meaning, their sensory qualities generally add nothing to the content of the message. But where there's sound, there's always going to be the likelihood of acoustic rhymes, assonances, and alliterations even if they're unintended. Like it or not, these incidental patterns can channel our thoughts into new paths. Thus, speech is always on the edge of poetry. Sometimes we really don't know where our thoughts are going until we hear what we say.[5]

This could be especially important when it comes to "inner speech," the internal monologues that many of us (if not all) engage in with only ourselves as audience. It's something of a puzzle to cognitive scientists that we think in words rather than "in thoughts." It's assumed by many linguists that when we generate speech, our brains take thoughts and turn them into words, and when we listen to speech, they take the words and turn them back into thoughts. Why, when we are thinking to ourselves, do we not do without the words and move directly from thought to thought? I have a suggestion. It's that if we were to take this shortcut, we would miss out on the rhyming possibilities and so ultimately think less creatively.

Given this potential of speech to produce accidental rhymes, it's worth noting that some human languages are more rhyme-prone than others. It's been said that Japanese words are made up of so few possible syllables that it's hard *not* to rhyme. Languages that make wide use of suffixal inflections (like Greek, Latin, and most Romance languages) also tend to produce frequent rhymes.

English—because of its lack of inflection, relatively loose grammar, exceptionally large number of syllables (6,949 as compared to 2,949 in French and 643 in Japanese),[6] and vast vocabulary—probably gives rise to fewer accidental rhymes than any other language. But there's a trade-off. In Japanese or French, where sound-rhymes are relatively common, they are much less attention-grabbing than in English, where their rarity marks them out as special. It may well be that because English rhymes have to be worked for and are relatively precious, English has proved historically to be such a richly inventive language, both in poetry and in informal speech.

It so happens that there's a similar national difference in garden design. Japanese and French gardens are characterized by their formality, symmetry, and control over nature, while English gardens are known for their natural appearance, informal layout, contrived wildness, and elements of surprise. The so-called linguistic relativity hypothesis that was popular in the 1960s claims that languages impose particular styles of thought on their users. Does it work for gardens too? In 1973, two English colleagues and I took part in a UNESCO symposium in France on aesthetics applied to the creation of the urban landscape. I talked about flowers, Peter Cook about the seaside, and Stephen Bann about garden cities. Our approach was quickly categorized as "L'approche anglaise."[7]

National differences aside, I suggest that the ever-present possibility of creative poetry, inside of language and out, provides an additional reason that a liking for rhyming beauty will have proved adaptive. It will have helped our ancestors to channel their thoughts into mapping the world not just as it is but *as it might be*.

The poet Joseph Brodsky wrote: "And this is what makes the whole enterprise of poetry so valuable for our species. For it is the principle of rhyme that enables one to sense that proximity between seemingly disparate entities. All these conjunctions of [Auden's] ring so true because they are rhymes. This closeness between objects, ideas, concepts, causes, and effects—this closeness, in itself, is a rhyme: at times, a perfect one, more frequently an assonance; or just a visual one. Having developed an instinct for these, you may have a better time with reality."[8]

Shelley said it even better. "The language [of poets] is vitally metaphorical; that is, it marks the before unapprehended relations of things."[9]

10 HOW MONKEYS ACQUIRE A NEW WAY OF SEEING

"Learning," said Aristotle, "is very agreeable, not only to philosophers but also to other men."[1] I'll come to other men, women, and children shortly. First, I want to describe some experimental findings that show how learning is agreeable to monkeys too. To use a more neutral term, it's "rewarding." The research is my own from fifty years ago.

In the 1970s, at the department of animal behavior at Cambridge University, I undertook a series of experiments to discover what monkeys—rhesus macaques—like to look at. The setup I employed was simple. The monkeys sat in a small dark chamber with a translucent screen at one end onto which slides or films could be projected (figure 10.1). When the subjects pressed and held down a button, they got either a picture or a blank white screen of roughly the same brightness. When they let go, the screen went dark. The next press and hold on the button gave them the alternative stimulus. Another press gave them the first stimulus, and so on in strict alternation.

Monkeys don't like to sit in complete darkness, so typically they kept the button pressed most of the time. But they also

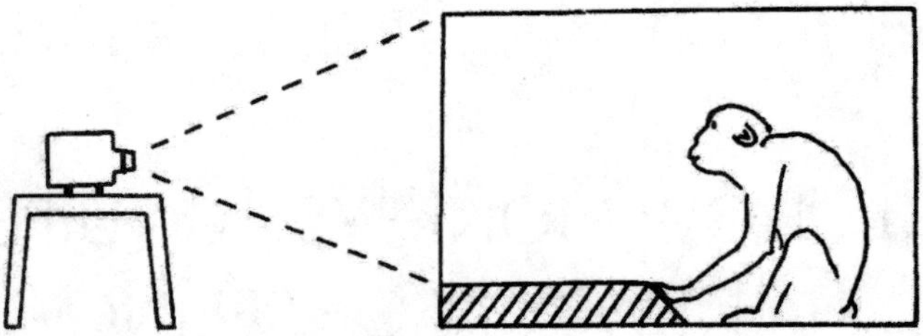

FIGURE 10.1
A visual preference testing chamber. Drawing by the author.

like change, so they would never stay with either the picture or the blank screen for long, letting go and quickly pressing again to get the alternative. By comparing the total time they stayed with the picture and blank screen, respectively, I was able to get a measure of how much they liked the picture.

The first findings were much as I expected.[2] The monkeys liked a picture of an animal more than a picture of a landscape. They liked an in-focus picture more than an out-of-focus picture. They liked colored pictures more than black-and-white pictures. They liked movies more than static pictures (they particularly liked Mickey Mouse cartoons). They liked movies played forward more than the same played backward. With static pictures, they usually lost interest within a minute or so, but as soon as the picture was replaced by another, their interest revived. With movies, their interest was generally maintained, but with a film loop that repeated after fifteen seconds, their interest waned.

In sum, the monkeys in this situation showed the greatest liking for pictures from which they had most to learn. In fact, I found that the drive to learn was so strong that they would choose to watch even when the experience was upsetting. I created some movies that I guessed would scare them—for example, a grotesque dancing mophead (figure 10.2). When

FIGURE 10.2
An image used to test monkeys' response to "scary pictures." From *Nature* 251, no. 5475 (October 11, 1974), cover. Photo © Nicholas Humphrey. Reproduced with permission from Springer Nature.

given the chance to watch this "horror movie" compared to the blank white screen, they stayed with the movie even while their hair stood on end and they urinated from fear.[3]

But *what* were the monkeys learning? How might they be *classifying* the things they saw on screen? In devising new experiments, I took my cue from the idea of a zoological taxonomist seeking out "rhyming animals."[4] I decided to investigate how the monkeys would respond to classes of animals they hadn't seen before.

The monkeys I was working with had been bred in captivity and had seen very little of the world at large. They had seen other monkeys and human beings. But I could assume they had never come across alien species such as cats, dogs, sheep, horses, or pigs. What would they make of them if they were to see pictures of these domestic animals for the first time?

To find out, I used a "dishabituation paradigm." As mentioned above, the monkeys' interest in a picture usually revived if, within a session, the picture changed—for example, from a photo of a sunflower to a photo of a car. But how big did a change have to be to reignite their interest? What if the second picture showed something they saw as being different but not *interestingly* different?

Would they, for example, see the differences between a cat and a dog as significant and so worth attending to but see the differences between two individual cats as relatively dull? How about the differences between two individual monkeys? In the case of their own species, would they be more discerning and see the differences between two individuals as an interesting rhyme rather than a mere repetition?

The pictures were colored photographs, showing a single animal against a relatively featureless background. The domestic animals were typical cats, dogs, sheep, horses, and pigs that varied in nonessential features such as size, age, coat color, bodily proportions, and facial expression. The monkeys were rhesus macaques like themselves (though never seen before) and varied in their looks. I tested all possible pairings, involving changes within species and across species.

The results were surprising.[5] When the picture changed from one species of domestic animal to another (for example, from dog to cat or from horse to pig), the monkeys' interest revived completely. But when the change was from a domestic animal to another individual of the same species (for example, from a dog to a different breed of dog or from a horse to a different horse), the revival was only about half as great. When, however, the change was from one individual *monkey* to another individual monkey, the revival was the same as for a change between two species of domestic animals.

In short, the results suggested that, for these monkeys, *monkeys as individuals* were interesting, *dogs as a class* were interesting, *cats as a class* and *horses as a class* were interesting, and so on, but dogs, cats, horses, and other nonmonkeys were relatively *uninteresting as individuals*.

This wasn't what I expected. While I guessed the monkeys might be particularly attentive to the differences between individual monkeys, I hardly expected them not to attend to the differences between individuals of other species. It was as if they were thinking, "When you've seen one member of the species, you've seen them all."

But a further surprise was to come. In the six months following the first experiment, I did other research, in the course of which these same monkeys got to see a feast of additional pictures, including seventy-five pictures of wild African animals (such as zebras, hippos, and leopards, many of which were not unlike the domestic animals), twenty-four pictures of landscapes, and a variety of nonrepresentational pictures. Most of these pictures were shown in the normal way, though thirty-two of the animals were upside down, a few were cut in half, and a few were "composite animals" made up, for instance, of the head of a hippo and the tail of a giraffe.

At the end, I repeated the first experiment to see if anything had changed. It had indeed. This time around, the subjects were just as interested when the picture changed from a domestic animal to another individual of the same species as they were when it changed from a monkey to a monkey. Apparently, the intervening experience had whetted their appetite for rhymes they had previously ignored. Now one dog rhymed with another dog after all.

What had brought this about? Although I hadn't predicted it, it was clear that as a result of seeing so many related examples, the monkeys had somehow "got their eye in." They now knew what to look for.

Intrigued by this evidence of what appeared to be increasing "cognitive acuity," I wondered how far it might go. If practice at seeing lots of other animals had deepened the monkeys' curiosity about individual animals of a strange species, was there some kind of practice that could make them look even more deeply into the peculiarities of individual monkeys?

I decided to find out by giving the subjects a chance to watch another monkey behaving in an odd way in a novel situation and then a chance to watch a different individual monkey doing the same. Would observing the first monkey inform what they looked for in the second?

The behavior I focused on was "private behavior"—what a monkey does when it thinks no one else is looking. When a monkey is out of sight of others, it will often get up to rather strange things. It will pull faces, play with its own body, do acrobatics, and so on—behavior that would be suppressed in a social situation. I guessed that other monkeys would be eager to be covert spectators of such a performance. More important, I thought that they might, if given the opportunity, grow increasingly sophisticated at seeing what was going on. That's to say, they might learn to see in the behavior of the monkey in private answers to questions that they would not at first have thought of asking.

I modified the testing chamber, replacing the screen with a television monitor. The TV camera was trained on an out-of-sight monkey in an isolated cage (figure 10.3). As I imagined,

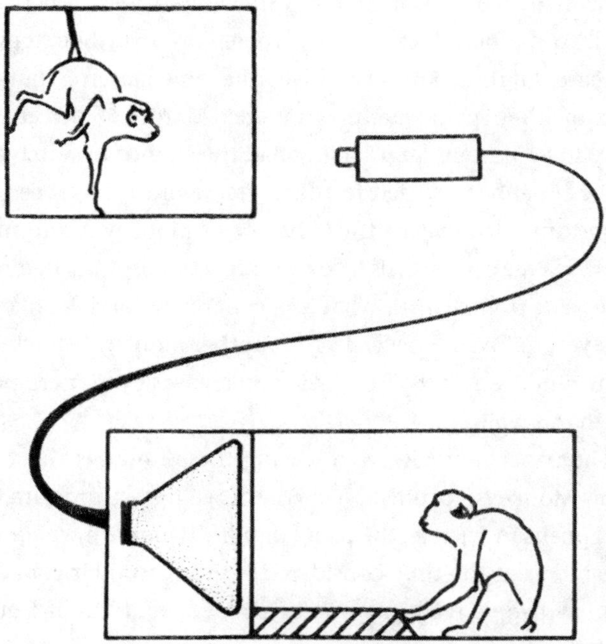

FIGURE 10.3
One monkey uses a TV screen to watch a second monkey acting up in private. Drawing by the author.

when the subjects controlling the button were able to switch to a view of the monkey in private, they loved it. Their interest remained at the same high level without diminishing over many days.

The experiment was designed as follows. Three monkeys were given the chance to watch monkey A in private, for ten-minute sessions twice a day for ten days, and their level of interest was measured. They were then given the chance to watch a second monkey, monkey B, under the same conditions for ten days. Next, they returned to watching A.

The results were as I hoped. The subjects' interest in monkey A remained at the same level for the first ten days. When A was switched to B, there was a stepwise increase to a higher level. And when A came back, there was a further stepwise increase. All three subjects showed the same pattern. The average time they spent watching A increased from 68 percent initially to 81 percent after having had the chance to watch B.

Presumably, what led to this increase must have been the opportunity to *compare* the behavior of monkey A and monkey B. If I may put words into the subjects' mouths, their reaction went from "Gosh, what a peculiar way for a monkey to behave"; to "Well, I never. Here's another monkey behaving in its own odd way"; to "The first monkey was even more peculiar than I realized."

The paper that I wrote reporting these findings was titled "How Monkeys Acquire a New Way of Seeing."[6] Unfortunately, as happens in science, the paper didn't rhyme with what other researchers at the time considered relevant to their concerns, and few people read it. I won't be repeating, then, if I quote from the discussion section:

> Suppose that human subjects were to be given the chance to view the private behaviour of another human being: the behaviour, let's

say, of a man in his bath. Suppose, specifically, that there were to be a daily television programme which from 10.00 to 10.15 each evening showed a cabinet minister in his bath. This programme, *Bath at Ten*, might feature different ministers on different days, starting perhaps with the following schedule: a week of the Chancellor of the Exchequer, followed by a week of the Home Secretary, followed by another week of the Chancellor of the Exchequer. If the results of the present experiment are anything to go by, we might predict that the audience rating for the programme would grow between the first week and the third. How, if it were so, should we account for this phenomenon?

At one level the two ministers would each present a similar spectacle: a naked man in a tub of water, washing himself. But there would almost certainly also be ways in which they were significantly different. Thus the Chancellor might be much dirtier than the Home Secretary, he might have a deeper bath, he might sit at the tap-end rather than the far end, he might use a sponge rather than a flannel, he might splash about much more, he might hum the National Anthem rather than "Jerusalem." . . .

Now, a naive viewer, during the first week of seeing the Chancellor, could hardly be expected to be in any way inquisitive about such differences. Why should he notice that the Chancellor was sitting by the taps if he had never seen someone sitting the other way round? Why should he notice that the Chancellor did not wash behind his ears if he had never seen someone else who did? But when the viewer came back to seeing the Chancellor after the intervening week of the Home Secretary, he would have become alert to a whole new range of possibilities. The microstructure of the bath-time behaviour would have been brought out by the comparative evidence.

Comparison pervades every level of perceptual classification. We see a bath as deep—deep relative to what? We see a man as dirty—dirty relative to what? And even when perceptual judgements could, logically, have some kind of absolute meaning, it takes comparison, psychologically, to bring that meaning into prominence. No one will see a coin as "heads" who has never seen one "tails," no one will see a man as naked who has never seen one clothed. The Lord God was right to be suspicious of Adam when he hid himself in the Garden of Eden: "And he said, Who told thee that thou wast naked? Hast thou eaten of the tree whereof I commanded thee that thou shouldest not eat?" The tree of knowledge is a branching decision tree, with *alternative* apples at the end of every branch.

I still think this captures it quite well.

* * *

The one scientist with whom my research at the time did strike a chord was my colleague in the department of animal behavior at Cambridge, Patrick Bateson.

He had been studying how newborn chicks learn to recognize their mothers. Shortly after hatching, chicks will "imprint" on any mother-object in the vicinity and become exclusively attached to it. But how do they avoid becoming hooked on just *one view* of this object? Bateson discovered that, for a brief period after imprinting on a particular object, the chick will actually look out for possible *variants* of it. In one of his experiments, the chick was first imprinted on a red (or yellow) flashing cylinder. It was then given access to a pedal, which when pressed changed the color to yellow (or red). He found that the chicks would actively step on the pedal to initiate the change.

Bateson interpreted this along the lines for which I've been arguing above. When you need to be able to identify an object whose appearance may vary over time, you can't rely on one view only. You must be familiar with possible rhymes. In his words:

> The ability to recognise a parent from all likely angles almost certainly requires more information than could possibly be acquired as the result of learning the characteristics of a single view of that

> parent. . . . If a young bird must recognise its parent from a variety of angles it must have first seen its parent from all those angles. This would in part be accomplished by rotations of the parent as it went about its business; but the process of attachment would be accelerated if, in addition, the young moved round the parent after familiarising themselves with one view.[7]

* * *

I'll mention one more finding with monkeys, which is an exception that proves the rule. I said I was surprised to discover that when the monkeys in my experiment first came across pictures of domestic animals, they paid little attention to individuality. But in fact, I had previously come up against an even more remarkable example of monkeys failing to discriminate between individual members of the same class.

As part of some earlier research, I attempted to teach monkeys to recognize the "odd one out" among a set of visual stimuli. The monkey was presented with an array of panels displaying four stimuli, three of which were the same and one different—for example, three stars and a square or three red circles and a green circle (figure 10.4). To receive a reward, they had to touch the one that differed.

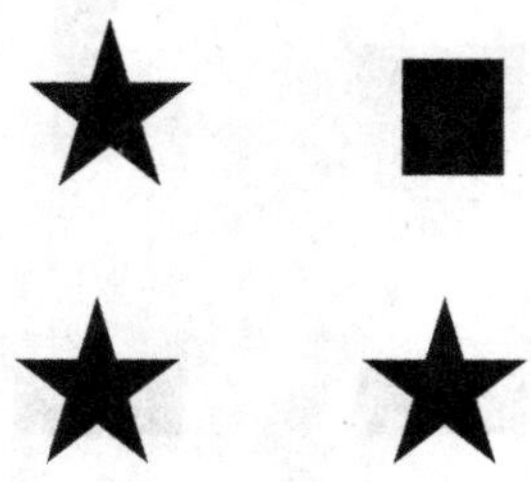

FIGURE 10.4
Visual oddity test with three stars and one square. Drawing by the author.

After extensive training with a range of different shapes, the monkeys apparently mastered the oddity principle so that when they were tested on transfer to a new example, they picked the odd one out first time. Inexplicably, there was one set of shapes that always confused them—horizontal and vertical bars (figure 10.5). When I tested them over and again with this set, they could never get it.

Much later, the explanation dawned on me. During training, my goal had been to teach the monkeys to choose the odd object represented on the panel. With all the training sets, one stimulus was indeed different from the other three in shape, size, or color.

However, with the new examples, I had slipped up. It hadn't occurred to me that a horizontal bar is actually the *same* shape—objectively—as a vertical one and is simply rotated by 90 degrees. Apparently, this similarity *had* occurred to the monkeys. They were classifying all bars, no matter what their orientation, as examples of the same kind of object. A bar is a bar.

In that case, it is no wonder they weren't able to choose the odd one out. In light of my later findings with pictures of animals, I can well believe that if I had shown the monkeys

FIGURE 10.5

Visual oddity test with three horizontal bars and one vertical bar. Drawing by the author.

in the oddity test three pictures of a particular pig and one of a different pig, they would have failed for the same reason. A pig is a pig.

But it's not just monkeys who, when it comes to classifying things, sometimes find it propitious to lump together things rather than split them. It was (or may have been) California's Governor Ronald Reagan who said about redwood trees: "A tree is a tree. How many trees do you need to see?"[8]

11 "LOOK AT ALL THE MILLOWS"

In the 1960s, psychologists working with human infants became interested in a phenomenon they called the response to "stimulus discrepancy." They observed that when infants less than a year old were exposed to a particular auditory or visual stimulus, the babies would orient toward a new version of the stimulus that differs moderately—not too much—from the original. Anticipating the present discussion, they suggested this is an instinctive response that in the real world will aid perceptual learning by bringing forward evidence about how objects vary in their properties.[1]

Unfortunately, this research, rather like my own with monkeys, remained in a backwater. Elizabeth Spelke's 2022 book, *What Babies Know: Core Knowledge and Composition*,[2] is a masterly survey of everything science has revealed in the past century about cognitive development in children. It has much to say about world models, but it makes no mention at all of rhyme.

But we really don't need scientific studies to make the point for humans. On all sides, we have the evidence of anecdote and common experience to demonstrate how people take pleasure in imposing cognitive order on the world. In this chapter, I'll discuss three outstanding examples. None of these will be news to you, but you may not have thought about them in this context.

NAMING

In the book of Genesis, God creates the animals and brings them to Adam in the Garden of Eden "to see what he would call them: and whatsoever Adam called every living creature, that was the name thereof" (figure 11.1).[3]

Adam, like my hypothetical zoologist, was a beginner. He cannot have known in advance what classes of animal he would find or what their distinguishing criteria would be. However, God gave Adam a helping hand. By delivering at

FIGURE 11.1
Adam Naming the Creation, engraving after Jan Luyken, 1732. Wellcome Collection, London. Public domain.

least two of every species, God provided a training set that gave Adam the opportunity to compare rhyming examples.

What was the purpose of this exercise in naming? Presumably, it was to help Adam build his mental model of Eden. At this point, Adam was the only language-speaking human in existence. Eve had not yet been created. So he did not yet need names to communicate with someone else. But names would have been central to his "language of thought," just as they are for us today.

As Carl Linnaeus, the eighteenth-century father of taxonomy, put it: "The first step in wisdom is to know the things themselves; this notion consists in having a true idea of the objects; objects are distinguished and known by classifying them methodically and giving them appropriate names. Therefore, classification and name-giving will be the foundation of our science."[4]

As we've seen, it is the foundation of *our* science too, by which I mean the theories each one of us arrives at about the nature of things in our surroundings. It's for this reason that human children have a thirst to learn names and to prove the power of their vocabulary with new examples. By the time they are eighteen months old, they are typically learning an average of two to five new words a day.

Children learn the common names for things from listening to the speech of adults, without much help from the adults themselves. But adults may also provide training sets in the form of picture books that serve as practical exercises in classification. The same animals—rabbits, hens, pigs—appear in the pictures again and again. "Where's the bunny?" asks the child's mother, and with a smile of satisfaction, the child points a finger to yet another rabbit that rhymes with those she has already seen.

When the name for an object is not available, a child will happily fill in the gap. The poet Richard Wilbur tells this story:

> I took my three-year-old son for a walk in the Lincoln woods. As we went along I identified what trees and plants I could. . . . After a while we came to a stretch of woods-floor thick with those three-inch evergreen plants one sees everywhere in New England woods, and I was obliged to confess I didn't know what to call them. My three-year-old stepped promptly into the breach. "They're millows," he told me. "Look at all the millows." No hesitation; no bravado; with a serene Adamite confidence he had found a name for something nameless and brought it under our verbal control. Millows they were.[5]

It may be most obvious in children, but adults too show an innocent delight in naming. A poem by Robert Bridges called "The Idle Flowers" mentions eighty-three different flowers by name in a poem only eighty-four lines long:

> I have sown upon the fields
> Eyebright and Pimpernel,
> And Pansy and Poppy-seed
> Ripen'd and scatter'd well.
>
> And silver Lady-smock
> The meads with light to fill,
> Cowslip and Buttercup,
> Daisy and Daffodil;
>
> King-cup and Fleur-de-lys
> Upon the marsh to meet
> With Comfrey, Watermint,
> Loose-strife and Meadowsweet:
>
> And all along the stream
> My care hath not forgot
> Crowfoot's white galaxy
> And love's Forget-me-not . . .[6]

Correspondingly, we think it comical when people make mistakes with names. The writer and politician A. P. Herbert tells a story against himself, again to do with flowers:

> "The anemias are wonderful," I said. My companion gave me a doubtful glance but said nothing. We walked on beside the herbaceous border. "And those arthritis, always so divine at this time of the year." Again the dubious glance, and again no utterance except an appreciative "Um." I came to the conclusion that the young lady knew no more about flowers than I do.[7]

But it's not a joke in older age, when loss of the ability to name becomes an early sign that a person's world model is dissolving.

COLLECTING

The delight we take in naming finds echoes in another remarkable aspect of human psychology—the passion for *collecting*. Whether the material of the collection is postage stamps, butterflies, or toy cars, at the heart of it lies the pleasure of completing a set. It's a pleasure that can become almost an addiction and take over people's lives.

In 1974, Charles Sibley, director of the Yale Peabody Museum, was fined $3,000 by the United States Fish and Wildlife Service for illegally importing birds' eggs from Great Britain. Sibley's prosecution was the result of detective work carried out by Richard Porter, an investigations officer of the Royal Society for the Protection of Birds and the scourge of British egg collectors. Porter himself expressed bewilderment at the activities of the men he hunted down. "Why do they do it?" he asked. "They camp out in appalling conditions. They carry out a desperately dangerous climb sometimes. Then they put the eggs in a cabinet with just themselves and a few friends to see them. They're just like kids."[8]

I know of only one scientist who has had insightful things to say about collecting, and that is the Russian physiologist Ivan Pavlov. In a 1916 lecture titled "The Reflex of Purpose," Pavlov characterized collecting as "the aspiration to gather together the parts or units of a great whole or of an enormous classification, usually unattainable" and continued:

> If we consider collecting in all its variations, it is impossible not to be struck with the fact that on account of this passion there are accumulated often completely trivial and worthless things, which represent absolutely no value from any point of view other than the gratification of the propensity to collect. Notwithstanding the worthlessness of the goal, everyone is aware of the energy, the occasional unlimited self-sacrifice, with which the collector achieves his purpose. He may become a laughing-stock, a butt of ridicule, a criminal, he may suppress his fundamental needs, all for the sake of his collection.[9]

The addiction can certainly strike in surprising places. My great-grandfather, who was a lecturer in philosophy at Cambridge University at the end of the nineteenth century, began collecting stamps as a child, moved on to collecting butterflies and birds' eggs as a young man, and was still devoted to this hobby when I came to know him at the age of ninety-five. By that time, his collections had grown so large that he had bought the house next door to be able to accommodate specially built chests of drawers.

Sigmund Freud amassed a huge collection of Roman, Greek, Egyptian, Assyrian, and Chinese figurines. These objects crowded his study and consulting room in Vienna. Edmund Engelman, who took photographs of this collection before Freud fled to England in 1938, described how "antiquities filled every available spot in the room. I was overwhelmed by the masses of figurines which overflowed every surface. To the left and right of the door were glass showcases filled with hundreds of antiquities. These were set up in several rows; every bit of cabinet space was filled." Freud's biographer Peter Gay noted that "The first and overpowering impression that Freud's habitat makes on the visitor is the profusion of things. . . . The sculptures have their assigned shelves and their glass cases, but they intrusively invade surfaces intended for other purposes: bookshelves, tops of cabinets, writing tables, even Freud's much used desk. The whole is an embarrassment of objects." But not an embarrassment to Freud. For him, it was more of a regimented kingdom, where every piece had its place: "The hundreds of statuettes are . . . arranged facing him at his desk in close-packed ranks like soldiers on parade."[10]

SPOTTING

More remarkable still—because of even less obvious value—is the time and expense people give to completing a collection not of tangible things but of merely fleeting *observations* of them.

Most children at one time or another have gone out armed with an observer book or an I-spy manual, with no grander purpose than merely to catch sight of a bird, toadstool, license plate, pub sign, or whatever. When I was a boy, I spent many hours "loco spotting"—standing on a railway bridge to record the class and number of each train engine as it went by. The craze may pass in childhood. But it may not. The "aero spotters," middle-aged as well as middlebrow, who used to throng the terminal roofs at Heathrow Airport provided big business for the London shops that catered for their needs. "The typical aero-spotter does nothing other than aero-spot," the proprietor of a shop for spotters told *The Guardian* newspaper. "He isn't married, or anything like that."[11]

And then there are the "twitchers." As described by *BBC Wildlife* magazine: "Twitching is the pursuit and observation of rare birds, and for many people it becomes a total obsession. It is a largely male pursuit and can be expensive—some twitchers even charter aircraft at short notice to reach far-flung destinations in the hope of crossing a species off their list. It can take over lives and ruin marriages, friendships, work prospects and wallets."[12]

For twitchers, checking off a rare bird brings a flurry of emotions. As one described it: "That rush of adrenaline is immediately followed by this remarkable sense of relief."[13] It's the rhyme that does it, that brings the sense of closure: "The cat . . . [wait for it] sat on the mat." Now we can go home.

What makes a collection a Collection? How does it differ from any mere aggregation of bizarre or precious objects? There are clear rules.

The first is that the things collected should fall within a strictly bounded category. A cigarette card has no place in a stamp collection, nor a snuffbox in a collection of thimbles, however rare and valuable each may be. The same goes for spotting. An aero spotter will take no interest in the hen harrier hovering above the Hawker Harrier aircraft on the runway.

But there's a second rule that in some ways is contrary to the first. For while all the members of a collection must be similar, they must not be so similar as to duplicate another. Fifty identical birds' eggs do not make an egg collection, and repeated sightings of the same railway engine bring no joy to the loco spotter. Collectors, within the limits of their chosen category, typically search for and prize variation. "Look at the crested titmouse eggs," said one of the egg collectors interviewed by Richard Porter: "This one belongs to the Scottish crested titmouse, this one to the Continental titmouse. Look at the difference."

Think of a stamp collection. Postage stamps are like man-made flowers. They can be divided into "species," of which the essential feature is the country of origin, while within each species there exist tantalizing differences—year issued, denomination, paper type, paper perforations, printing process, subject. The philatelist (he has an important-sounding title) sets to work to classify them (figure 11.2). He arranges his stamps in an album, with a section for the species of each country. The stamps on each page rhyme with each other, while they have distant rhymes with those on other pages.

But Pavlov was right: Stamp collecting is ultimately a worthless activity. As we've moved through the examples—from an infant learning to name pictures in a book, to a twitcher

FIGURE 11.2
François Barraud, *Le Philatéliste*, 1929. Wikimedia Commons.

ticking off sightings of birds, to a philatelist sticking stamps in an album—we've moved further from activities that bring any practical benefits. Arguably, they are all examples of the pleasures to be had from taking cognitive control of a particular corner of the world, but with each example this corner would seem to be less relevant to human needs. If the love of classifying things has evolved to help people learn what they *need to know* about their world, collecting might seem to be merely a playful waste of time, bordering on maladaptive.

From an evolutionary viewpoint, this is not really surprising. We might compare the pleasure people get from "playing with rhyme" with the pleasure they get from "playing with sex." Although sex has a clear biological function related to reproduction, nonreproductive sex is undoubtedly enjoyable. In fact, most human sexual activity, and the most exotic forms of it, can be said to be merely "sex for sex's sake." And perhaps "classification for classification's sake" is not so different.

Nor should we be surprised if, in the modern world, the urge to classify sometimes gets out of hand. Just as humans are liable to overindulge in eating if they live in a sweet shop or in watching pornography when it's easily available online, so they may be sucked in by the challenge presented by man-made artifacts, such as postage stamps and airplanes that fall neatly into quasi-natural categories. These artifacts provide what ethologists call a *superstimulus*. The aero spotter "who isn't married or anything like that" is behaving like a seagull who broods a gigantic china egg in preference to the real thing.

There's no question that an addiction to collecting may be a liability. And yet there could also be a beneficial side to it. Even if we do not learn anything of practical value from the activity of classifying things that are of no earthly use to us, we may still be *learning how to learn* about the world in general.

Consider the parallel with music, an even better example of a cognitive superstimulus. Music serves not only as an opportunity to take pleasure in rhyming structures but also as a *guided exercise* in classification. Sonata form illustrates this perfectly. We are walked through the rhyming structure of the soundscape, as on a path through a botanical garden. And all the while, we are learning for ourselves how to structure the evidence wherever and whenever we need to acquire genuinely useful information.

Compared to music, stamp collecting is at best a minor art form. Nonetheless, I dare say my great-grandfather's hobby honed the tools of his trade as a logician.[14]

12 ABOUT UGLINESS

"Obscurity," in the words of philosopher David Hume, "is painful to the mind as well as to the eye; but to bring light from obscurity, by whatever labour, must needs be delightful and rejoicing."[1] Right. But it does indeed work both ways. The flip side of beauty is ugliness. Just to the extent that humans—and animals too—take pleasure in making sense of their world, they are bound to find it distressing when they are unable to do so.

It will be bad enough if they simply cannot make out what's going on simply because the picture is blurry or unstable. The monkeys in my visual preference experiments positively disliked movies that were out of focus.[2] But it will be much worse if they find that what they are looking at is *conceptually obscure* because it contains things that clash with their world model. Thus, the monkeys found the movie of a dancing mophead terrifying, because, I guess, it was in-between a mop and a face. They responded similarly to a movie of a ball of paper going up in flames and turning to smoke, because they had never seen paper consumed by a flame.

When constructing objects to scare the monkeys for this study, I took my cue from research on chimpanzees conducted in the 1940s by Donald Hebb. Hebb proposed on theoretical grounds that "Fear occurs when an object is seen which is like familiar objects in enough respects to arouse habitual processes of perception, but in other respects arouses incompatible processes."[3] He saw this, for example, in how young chimps in his laboratory reacted to "anomalous" humans. "Dr. R. and Mr. T. are regular attendants in a chimpanzee nursery; the infants are attached to both, and eagerly welcome being picked up by either. Now, in full sight of the infants. Dr. R. puts on Mr. T.'s coat. At once he evokes fear reactions identical with those made to a stranger, and just as strong. An unfamiliar combination of familiar things, by itself, can therefore produce a violent emotional reaction."[4]

In her classic book *Purity and Danger: An Analysis of Concepts of Purity and Pollution*, the anthropologist Mary Douglas argued on similar lines that humans find both "formlessness" and "contradictory formations" cognitively threatening. Thus, for example, people brought up to have a binary attitude to sex may feel threatened by individuals who blur the distinctions between male and female. Homosexual love may be literally "a love that dare not speak its name." In the case of the Ulas children, whom I described playing on a Turkish beach on the first page of this book, their neighbors threw stones at them to keep the "half-humans, half-animals" at bay.

To illustrate her general thesis, Douglas homed in on the "taboos of Leviticus," the Bible's listing of unclean animals that must not be eaten: "In general, the underlying principle of cleanness in animals is that they shall conform fully to their class. Those species are unclean which are imperfect members of their class, or whose class itself confounds the general scheme of the world."[5] The basis for the prohibition is made explicit in the biblical text. Edible land animals include those (such as sheep and cows) that both chew the cud and have cloven hooves. But the camel and the hare are unclean, because they chew the cud but do not part the hoof; likewise, the swine, because it parts the hoof but does not chew the cud. Edible water animals are those that have both fins and scales; eels are unclean because they have fins but no scales.

Things that cross boundaries and challenge the established order are conceptually disturbing. If the problem arises simply because our taxonomy is incomplete, we may be able to resolve it by shoehorning potential outliers into existing categories. A *Punch* cartoon (figure 12.1) nicely illustrates this way of coping. A lady has arrived at the station with an unusual array of pets. The railway's rules say that dogs must be charged for but all other animals travel for free: "Station Master say,

FIGURE 12.1
"Zoology," *Punch*, March 6, 1869. Public domain.

Mum, as cats is 'dogs,' and rabbits is 'dogs,' and so's parrots; but this ere 'tortis' is an insect, so there ain't no charge for it!"

But we have several other ways of protecting our existing worldview. One creative way of dealing with objects that appear to break the rules of the normal world is to remove them altogether from contention with normality by assigning them to a special category where the rules are suspended—an out-of-bounds "holy space."

A space of special relevance to our discussion is that of "art." Gertrude Stein tells of her initial dismay when she first saw cubist paintings in the 1910s: "It is very difficult now that everybody is so accustomed to everything to give an idea of the kind of uneasiness felt when one first looked at all these pictures on these walls. . . . Now I was confused and I looked and I looked and I was confused."[6] When Igor Stravinsky's ballet *The Rite of Spring* premiered in Paris in 1913, many men and women in the audience were so outraged by the avant-garde score and Vaslav Nijinsky's choreography that they took the performance as an insult to themselves and to society at large. But times and concepts soon moved on. The outrageous style received a new name, "Modernism," and in the process, the offending artworks were rendered safe. "Modern art" became art that is intended to be anomalous and even slightly mad. As Pablo Picasso said, "Nature and art being two different things cannot be the same thing. Through art we express our conception of what nature is not."[7]

In cognitive psychology, special attention has been given to a particular class of rule-defying objects—the so-called impossible objects, of which the most famous is the Penrose triangle. Again, we have a name for such a thing, it's a *visual illusion*. And again, the name tames it and puts it in its place. We expect illusions to be illusory. Of course, illusions and

FIGURE 12.2
The Penrose triangle. Drawing by the author.

reality being different things cannot be the same thing. By this conceptual trick, we get to *own* the anomaly rather than having to confront it as an alien presence. But think how disturbing we might find the drawing shown in figure 12.2 if we weren't able to quarantine it in this way.

How would earlier generations of humans have dealt with this image before they had this work-around? It's often assumed that impossible objects are a recent discovery. But the same design is at the center of a religious motif known as "the three hares" that has been known to humans for more than a thousand years (figure 12.3). The earliest example appears on the roof a Buddhist cave temple in China from about AD 700. It was introduced by the Mongols to central Europe and became widely incorporated into Jewish and Christian iconography. In England, it occurs in the roof bosses of many medieval churches, especially in the county of Devon.[8]

The hare as an animal has since ancient times been regarded as an in-between creature. As we saw, it was included in the list of unclean animals in Leviticus on the grounds (mistaken, as it happens) that it chews the cud. But there was also a folk belief that the hare was a hermaphrodite and could procreate without a mate. This led to the rumor that it could give birth

FIGURE 12.3
The three hares. Drawn by the author from a traditional design.

to offspring without losing its virginity and so, in Christian contexts, to an association with the Virgin Mary.

We don't know what ancient people made of the strange design or even what they called it. Maybe they made a point of not giving it a name. But its power must surely have lain in its apparent impossibility. Eighteenth-century synagogues in Germany show a riddle alongside the motif: "Three hares sharing three ears, yet every one of them has two." And the fact that this design occurs only in religious contexts—churches, temples, synagogues, psalters, holy books—suggests it has always been regarded as an emblem of the supernatural.

This is the other safe place to which people can conveniently assign anomalies. What's counternatural (against nature) becomes reclassified as supernatural (above nature)—the realm of the immortals and the gods. In fact, by reverse logic, this is a realm where anomaly becomes the rule. That's how you recognize that you are leaving earth behind. So, for example, in Christianity there are the in-your-face exceptions to the world order that are central to many Bible stories, as in the virgin birth or the resurrection. In Buddhism, there are reincarnation and the cycle of rebirth. And more subtly, there are the teasing contradictions of Zen koans: "What is the sound of one hand clapping?" "Asking what Buddha is, is like hiding loot in one's pocket and declaring oneself innocent." "'Manjursi, why do you not enter the gate?' 'I do not see myself as outside. Why enter?'"

For Christians, openness to supernatural events is a test of faith. For Buddhists, meditation on riddles is explicitly recommended as a path to "enlightenment." This reveals a surprising aspect of human psychology. While our first response to being confronted by something that challenges common sense is often anxiety, the next can be the willing suspension of our critical faculties. There can be joy to be had in abandoning the quest for answers when none are within reach.

You might think that a feeling of cognitive helplessness would—and should—be deeply distressing to us, and it usually will be. But there are certainly times and places where we're happy to throw in the towel and return to the state of childhood, when we could trust our parents to do the understanding for us.

Enlightenment, in this sense, means not so much being struck by the light of knowledge as being relieved of the burden of needing it. It can work for Western intellectuals just as it does for Eastern monks. Philosopher Colin McGinn, for example, reacted to his own "discovery" that the solution to the mind-body problem was beyond human comprehension (although perhaps not beyond God's) with a sigh of acceptance: "That's all right, then; now I can get on with something else."[9]

What does it take to make us feel cognitively overwhelmed? Contrived impossibilities, can do it—miracles, apparent contradictions. But so, sometimes, can the world taken just as it is. Isaac Newton, as a mathematician, may have stood on the shoulders of giants, but he confessed that nonetheless the natural world made him feel humble and small: "to myself I seem to have been only like a boy playing on the seashore . . . whilst the great ocean of truth lay all undiscovered before me."

Newton's image of the seashore is peculiarly appropriate. It's in just such natural settings—under the starry sky, in the mountains, at the edge of a canyon, under the dome of a cathedral—that we all may feel that the world surpasses our ability to make sense of it. But confronted by something that appears to be grand beyond our comprehension, we do not panic or try to escape. We feel *awe*—a mix of wonder, reverence, and calm submissiveness. We're content to be part of a cosmic order of which our own ignorance makes it all the more impressive.[10] The feeling is accompanied by a sense of smallness—a shrinking of the body and the self. This in turn can lead to a sense of becoming one with nature—and the rest of humanity.[11]

Yet awe, however good it feels and however morally uplifting in the moment, is an emotion that should be kept under control. A chronic state of awe would be dispiriting and intellectually unhealthy. "The world is vast and wide," goes another Zen koan: "Why do you put on your robes at the sound of a bell?" Why live, as a monk, in "the cloud of unknowing" when the ocean of truth lies undiscovered but—we may always hope—discoverable?

13 COGNITION FIRST

In exploring the connections between rhyme and cognition, we've left behind the other domains where, as we saw at the start of the book, people actually benefit in practical ways from living among rhyming objects. As I said earlier, evolutionary psychologists have generally assumed that it was these practical benefits that were primarily responsible for the evolution of a rhyme detector and a generalized attraction to rhyming things. What mattered was the "real excellence of the objects" that people encountered.

Now that we've seen so many ways in which the *experience of rhyme can be its own reward at a cognitive level*, I want to return to my counterproposal—that what mattered primarily was "the valuable effects of the experience." In short, cognitive beauty led the way. Our distant ancestors first developed a general interest in the beauty of rhyme because of the cognitive rewards, and only *as a result of this* did the practical benefits of living alongside rhyming things come into focus.

Early humans could have been attracted for cognitive reasons purely to the *look* of another individual who moved rhythmically and had a symmetrical body or to the *look* of a shell necklace that the individual offered as a gift and then, by way of this, discovered that such an individual was likely to make a good life partner. They could have been attracted purely to the *look* of places full of rhyming plants and animals and, by way of this, discovered that such places offer security. They could have been attracted to the *look* of flints with a balanced symmetrical shape and, by way of this, discovered that such things make good blades.

In support of the idea that this was the order of events, it's worth pointing out that the evolutionary sequence—in which the pursuit of beauty for its own sake has led to the discovery of things with practical value—is a pattern that has occurred repeatedly in the history of human cultural invention. Gunpowder was used in China for fireworks before it found use in weaponry. Mathematicians invented complex numbers (involving the square root of minus one) for the beauty of the mathematics before engineers adopted them for telecommunications. The research that led to discovery of the structure of DNA was, as Crick described it, "a mad pursuit" before it became the key to modern medicine.

But there's a special reason for believing something like this happy sequence could have occurred with rhyme. In the settings that evolutionary psychologists have chiefly considered, the practical advantages that flowed from "innocently" following the lead of cognitive beauty would very likely have had a *social amplifier*. When one person liked the look of something because of its rhymes, the chances are that other people independently would have liked it too. And this convergence in taste between *yourself* and others might have added considerably to the benefits to be gained from seeking out what *you* considered beautiful. Thus, beautiful individuals would have made even better partners for us because other people liked the look of them. Beautiful places would have offered even more security to us because other people congregated there. Beautiful flint tools would have been even more worth selecting and refining because other people thought highly of them and we could trade them.

You might think this social amplifying effect would not have counted for much compared to other direct benefits. However, because humans are the extraordinarily interdependent creatures that they are, I reckon it could have been highly significant. Indeed, it raises another interesting possibility. Given that having a common interest in a particular set of things brings people together and that social interaction is of itself a benefit to humans, this means that the love of rhyme could have proved adaptive even if it was never associated with any more specific outcomes. When people come together at a garden party, at a musical event, or at a stamp club, unexpected adaptive consequences flow from it. It's like gathering round a campfire. "There's no disputing tastes," they say. But if having the *same* tastes as others brings people together, this could be part of the reason for having tastes at all.

A similar dynamic—where a trait is adaptive because others share it—has certainly been game changing in another case: namely, the evolution of courtship displays in animals by what's called *sexual selection*. When, for example, a male animal has an external feature that a female likes the look of (say, the eyespot on a peacock's tail), one of the benefits to her of choosing him as a mate is that her own male offspring will have a good chance of inheriting this feature and so of appealing to other females who like the same things she does. The same logic applies, *mutatis mutandis*, when a male chooses a female. As Darwin recognized, almost any bodily or behavioral trait can in principle be elevated in this way to become the target of sexual attraction, with the trait then becoming exaggerated because of positive feedback.

But the process has to start somewhere. And, just as I've suggested may happen for humans in other areas of interest, the obvious way for the process to get going is when courting animals home in on a particular feature that they notice because it is already cognitively attractive: They notice it, that is, because it's noticeable. This would explain why courtship displays are so often built up from rhyming elements—the pirouetting dance of a great crested grebe, the harmonies of a blackbird's song, the symmetry of a stag's antlers—that were cognitively attractive to begin with.

Returning to humans, if I'm right that cognition led the way across all domains of beauty—the beauty of a sunset, an axe, a baby, a symphony—it means these have more in common than, as theorists, we might have dared imagine. It's not just, as Hopkins proposed, that all beauty may be called rhyme. It's that all beauty began with rhyme in evolution. And probably involves the same machinery in the brain.

* * *

This is of considerable interest theoretically. It opens the door on a possible feature of human psychology that has so far been missing from our discussion: that people do indeed feel a unique kind of emotion when they encounter cognitive beauty (even if is mixed in with more down-to-earth pleasures that frequently come next).

"Aesthetic emotion" is a phrase I haven't used since chapter 1, where I suggested that there is something special about our response to beauty that sets it apart from other kinds of enjoyment. This idea, once taken for granted by writers from Aristotle to Thomas Reid, is no longer so popular as it once was. It was dismissed by philosopher Nelson Goodman as "aesthetic phlogiston."[1] But for reasons I'll now explain, I believe the older view may be scientifically correct.

14 VALUE IN A WORLD OF FACTS

Aristotle called learning "very agreeable." The psychologist Alison Gopnik has gone further and called the pleasure of arriving at an explanation "orgasmic."[1] Most people would agree that seeing how things fit together is, at the very least, intellectually satisfying.

However, aesthetic pleasure is surely more than intellectual. You'll recall how, in Hopkins's "Platonic Dialogue," the student expressed dissatisfaction with what he considered to be the professor's overly logical approach: "I am sure there is in the higher forms of beauty . . . something mystical, something I don't know how to call it. Is not there now something beyond what you have explained?"

When this came up earlier, I said I thought the student had a point and I hoped that later in the book we might be in a better position to say what the "something" beyond rhyme could be—perhaps something that speaks to broader human interests. I now have a proposal that I want to try on you. It's that there is something about rhyme that is *morally satisfying*. And this applies not only to the rhyme that underlies the "higher forms of beauty" but all the way through to "The cat sat on the mat."

My starting point is the idea of "belonging." I defined rhyme at the start in terms of family relationships: Two entities rhyme when we recognize that, while they differ, they belong together. This is precisely what makes rhyme such a good lead to the kinds of things that exist in the world. What I now want to suggest is that belonging is intrinsically a *value-laden* concept. When we bring two rhyming things together in our head, we are recognizing that, given the rules that govern the world, this is the way it *ought to* be: These things somehow deserve to be joined up.

There is a related concept that was introduced into the scientific study of perception by the Gestalt psychologists in the 1930s. They called it by the German word *pragnanz,* often translated as "goodness." It refers to our tendency to perceive things in accordance with psychologically compelling laws that have evolved to bring perception into correspondence with physical reality. Figure 14.1 illustrates the six Gestalt laws or principles:

- *Law of similarity:* Similar things tend to appear grouped together. In the figure, you probably see two sets of two separate rows rather than just a collection of dots.
- *Law of good figure:* When you are presented with a set of ambiguous or complex objects, your brain makes them appear as simple as possible. Thus, when you look at the Olympic logo, you see overlapping circles rather than an assortment of curved, connected lines.
- *Law of proximity:* Things that are close together seem more related than things spaced farther apart.
- *Law of continuity:* Points that are connected by straight or curving lines are seen in a way that follows the smoothest path.

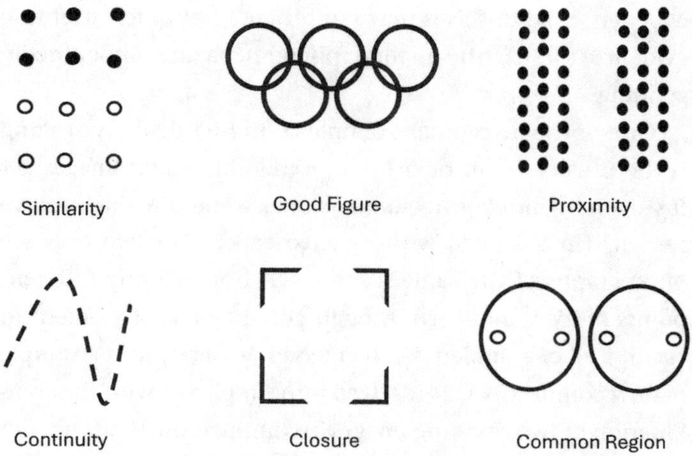

FIGURE 14.1
The six Gestalt laws of perception. Drawings by the author.

- *Law of closure:* Elements are seen as belonging to the same group if they complete a meaningful entity. Thus, in the figure, you see the shape of a square.
- *Law of common region:* When elements are located in the same closed region, they are seen as belonging to the same group. In the figure, you see each of the four dots as belonging with its mate within the two large circles, even though the two central dots are closer to each other than they are to their mates within their own circle.

It's as if certain patterns in the visual input create "lines of force" in the mind that tend in a particular direction toward a final resting state. Elements that belong together find each other automatically and coalesce to make larger wholes. Indeed, the Gestalt theorists believed there are electrical force fields in the brain that create these psychological effects, there being an *isomorphism* between these fields and mental experience. Be this as it may (and there's not much scientific evidence for it), the mental phenomena are undoubtedly genuine.

One of the perceptual examples I find particularly striking is the phenomenon of *stereopsis*, when binocular images get fused into a single three-dimensional scene. I'm sure you've seen it demonstrated with a stereoscope. Your two eyes see photographs of the same scene taken from slightly different points of view, and then, though you may take a moment to "get it," all of a sudden depth emerges. It's a beautiful example of how complexity gets resolved into simplicity, with the combination of two rhyming images becoming more than the sum of its parts.

Remarkably enough, stereopsis works even when there are no depth cues at all in the images taken separately. With figure 14.2, you would have no idea that the combination of the two images will reveal a three-dimensional object until you try it. You can try it without a stereoscope simply by crossing your eyes until the images appear to be superimposed. It may take some practice, but when you succeed, a square will suddenly emerge apparently cut out of the background.

FIGURE 14.2
Béla Julesz's random-dot stereograms. Public domain.

The Gestalt psychologists believed that similar forces leading to a "good" outcome operate not only in perception but also at more abstract levels of cognition, including problem-solving. If the parts that together would form the solution to a puzzle are present in the thought field, the answer may "pop up" of its own accord. Wolfgang Köhler saw evidence of this in his famous example of a chimpanzee "thinking out" how to reach a banana hanging from the ceiling. The chimpanzee saw the banana, saw a pile of boxes on which he could stand, and *saw* the solution, The thinking-out happened *without thinking,* as a result of autochthonous forces in the brain (figure 14.3).[2]

Köhler went further with this theorizing. In 1934, he delivered the William James Lectures at Harvard University under the title *The Place of Value in a World of Facts.*[3] There he introduced a new concept that he called "requiredness." He meant the concept to cover "all facts without exception in which beyond mere existence and occurrence there is an 'ought' or

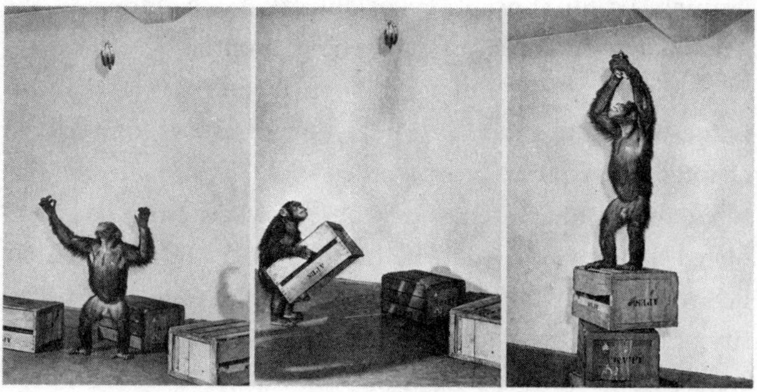

FIGURE 14.3
The chimpanzee Sultan seeing a solution to the banana puzzle. From Wolfgang Köhler, *The Mentality of Apes,* trans. Ella Winter (Kegan Paul, Trench, Trubner & Co., 1925), 174. Public domain.

'ought not.'" "Certain facts," he wrote, "do not only happen or exist, but issuing as vectors in parts of contexts, extend towards others with a quality of acceptance or rejection."[4] He believed that requiredness is characteristic not only of mental phenomena but of social, biological, physical, and mathematical phenomena as well. In fact, requiredness is part and parcel of the way the universe is constituted.

The phrase "the place of value in a world of facts" caught on (and was made the title of a Nobel symposium in 1969), but the idea of requiredness, as such, never became a successful meme. By 1947, when Köhler published *Gestalt Psychology: An Introduction to New Concepts in Modern Psychology*, a revised version of his famous 1929 book, he seemed to have lost confidence in what he earlier proposed (the words "requiredness" and "value" do not appear in the index).

It's true there was always something a bit hand-wavy about requiredness ("something mystical, something I don't know how to call it"—though he did). However, in my view, it's a lastingly useful concept, even if it needs amending. In the field of aesthetics, we can hardly do without it.

Central to all theories of beauty is the proposition that this is the way things ought to be. I quoted Ernst Gombrich in chapter 1: "What an artist worries about as he plans his pictures, makes his sketches, or wonders whether he has completed his canvas, is . . . whether he has got it 'right.'" Clive Bell wrote in similar vein: "The artist has got to feel the necessity of making his work of art 'right.' It will be 'right' when it expresses his emotion for reality. . . . Certain combinations are perceived to be right and necessary, and our perception of their rightness and necessity is moving."[5]

But it really is not so different when we're talking about beauty in nature. When we see how a sunset, a flowery meadow, or a theorem of Euclid is apparently so well balanced and harmonious, we're moved by the realization that nature has got it right. Which is to say—for what else could this mean?—*right by us*.

I think this is where Köhler bypasses evolutionary psychology. He believed that requiredness is a feature of the physical world, independent of human beings—indeed, that value can be found in facts alone. But I'd say requiredness must be as much a human concept as a physical one. It comes down to two basic truths—the *material truth* that the world is required by its physical constitution to be orderly and law-abiding and the *psychological truth* that the world is required by our mental models to be orderly and law abiding.

Bringing these together, it's as if there's a "social contract" between us and nature. Provided nature does her bit to follow the rules, we'll do ours to recognize her for it. And it's precisely this, I suggest, that adds the moral dimension to beauty.

The philosopher Roger Scruton has expressed a similar idea: "The experience of beauty tells us that 'we are at home in the world, that the world is already ordered in our perceptions as a place fit for the lives of beings like us.'"[6] The German poet Novalis wrote: "Philosophy is really Homesickness; the wish to be everywhere at home."[7]

According to Wilfred Sellars, "The aim of philosophy, abstractly formulated, is to understand how things in the broadest possible sense of the term hang together in the broadest possible sense of the term."[8] But let's be clear: The aim of evolved human cognition is exactly the same.

* * *

Gestalt theory provides a key to the dynamics of the aesthetic emotion that I drew attention to at the beginning. There are many times when, in contemplating beauty, we find ourselves engaging not with the final answer but with the *promise* of one, the hint of an outcome as yet unborn—what Samuel Taylor Coleridge described as being "on the brink of a fruition still denied" and Jorge Luis Borges as "the imminence of a revelation which does not occur."[9]

While the German word *pragnanz* may be translated as "goodness," another meaning is equally pertinent—"pregnant," waiting to give birth. Many Gestalt phenomena do indeed take time to gestate. You can see this with stereopsis, where in may take several seconds for the three-dimensional pattern to emerge. The same is true of puzzle pictures, such as the hidden man (figure 14.4), where it may take much longer before the mental force fields coalesce in an aha! solution (although once they've done so, it can't be undone). And Köhler's

FIGURE 14.4
The hidden man. Drawing by the author, based on M. L. J. Abercrombie, *The Anatomy of Judgement: An Investigation into the Processes of Perception and Reasoning* (Hutchinson, 1960).

chimps took a few minutes to solve the problem of reaching the banana.

Rhyming verse provides a paradigm example of how the promise of an answer affects us. Take a simple limerick. We know there's a rhyme coming but not what it will be:

> There was an old man of Peru
> Who watched his wife making a stew.
> But once by mistake
> In a stove she did bake
> That unfortunate man of Peru.

Here we have to wait only for a moment for the resolution. But in life, we are often left on hold much longer. The human brain, as we saw, is a prediction engine that—on the basis of its world model—continually makes a best guess about what's coming next (and when its guess is off, adjusts the settings of its model). In effect, *the world is a poem*, and we are constantly anticipating how the next line will end.

In affect too. Psychologists Thomas Armstrong and Brian Detweiler-Bedell have summed it up perfectly:

> The experience of beauty . . . reflects the prospect of understanding something novel and particularly meaningful. . . . Beauty presages understanding before one's cognitive faculties can be certain that an object or experience will yield to any coherent conceptual representation. Beauty is not discerned. Rather, it is the felt prospect of cognitively representing and achieving processing mastery over a challenging object or experience.[10]

Let's call it *pregnant uncertainty*. The emotion is notably different from the feeling of awe. Awe involves giving up. Pregnant uncertainty involves hanging in there, even at the risk of failing. Depending on our attitude to risk, such moments of cognitive uncertainty may supply our greatest aesthetic pleasure.

15 SIGNIFICANT FORM IN NATURE

I want to air another issue central to aesthetic emotion. If the perception of rhyming beauty is tinged with a feeling of moral satisfaction—the feeling that things are coming together in the required way, something for which we feel gratitude—it raises a question. Required by what? Gratitude to whom? Whom do we have to *thank* for bringing us home?

It's easy to answer in the case of man-made works of art. When the thing of beauty has been created by a human artist, there will be an obvious direction for our thoughts to take. We should credit the person of the artist with having seen the rhyming structure and represented it in a way we can appreciate. It's to him or her that we owe the emotional experience.

Clive Bell, in his book *Art,* made the viewer's relationship with the artist the basis for his theory:

> That there is a particular kind of emotion provoked by works of visual art, and that this emotion is provoked by every kind of visual art, pictures, sculptures, buildings, pots, carvings, textiles, &tc., &tc., is not disputed, I think, by anyone capable of feeling it. . . . Lines and colours combined in a particular way, certain forms and

> relations of forms, stir our aesthetic emotions. These relations and combinations of lines and colours, these aesthetically moving forms, I call "Significant Form."[1] . . . [Significant form] moves us so profoundly because it expresses the emotion of its creator.[2]

Bell saw it working something like this. The artist has a special gift of being able to go behind appearances and discover the "deeper reality" of things. His skill consists in translating this reality into a *readable* form in paint, clay, marble, or other medium. When we contemplate the work, we are privileged to be able to share in his discoveries. The artist, in that evocative phrase of Browning, "lends his mind [and his heart] out."

Paul Cézanne described what I believe Bell meant: "To love a painting, one must . . . descend with the painter into the dim tangled roots of things, and rise again . . . steeped in the light of them."[3]

But wait. This is clearly not going to work in every case. If aesthetic emotion involves communication with an artist, it follows that *only* man-made examples of beauty can give rise to it. When the object is not man-made, this kind of communication would seem to be impossible in principle. To whom do we owe our feelings for natural beauty?

Now, far from seeing this as a difficulty, Bell himself embraced this conclusion. It explains, he says, the "curious but undeniable fact" that

> what I call material beauty (e.g. the wing of a butterfly) does not move most of us in at all the same way as a work of art moves us. It is beautiful form, but it is not significant form. It moves us, but it does not move us aesthetically. It is tempting to explain the difference . . . by saying that significant form conveys to us an emotion felt by its creator and that [material] beauty conveys nothing.[4]

Thus, by Bell's account, none of the examples we've considered earlier in this book of people taking pleasure in the "material" beauties of nature would count as cases of aesthetic emotion. Yet I don't hesitate to say that this seems to be factually wrong. It's at odds with my own experience—and I expect yours. To the contrary, material beauty does, sometimes, move us in very much the same way that a work of art does.

Consider, for example, how the English naturalist Richard Jefferies describes his response to a scene unmediated by any artist:

> I looked at the hills, at the dewy grass, and then up through the elm branches to the sky. In a moment all that was behind me, the house the people, the sounds, seemed to disappear, and to leave me alone. Involuntarily I drew a long breath, then I breathed slowly. My thought, or inner consciousness, went up through the illumined sky, and I was lost in a moment of exaltation. . . . I was absorbed; I drank the beauty of the morning.[5]

Without doubt, this *resembles* the response to a work of art.

To square Bell's theory with my own, I want to return to a feature of human psychology that I brought up earlier in the book. Suppose people were to be *under the illusion* that an artist is responsible? Could this result in natural beauty acquiring significant form, as it were, by the back door?

Why would I even want to go this way? It's because I can't but agree with Bell about a crucial issue. In the case of man-made works of art, the facts of aesthetic experience clearly speak to the importance of the "psychic presence" of the artist. Unless we accept that the case of natural beauty is really very different—which I don't—there has to be a way of putting an illusory artist into nature.

* * *

There's one compelling reason for thinking Bell is right about works of art. This is that our response is critically dependent on the back story of who made it. The evidence exists at several levels.

For a start, we may not attend to the work at all until it's been pointed out to us *as* "art." Henry David Thoreau said: "We do not enjoy poetry fully unless we know it to be poetry."[6] And the same goes for man-made art in general. We are drawn to look at a framed picture in a gallery where we might miss it entirely if we were to come across the same scene unframed outside. As Robert Browning wrote in the poem I've already quoted: "We're made so that we love / First when we see them painted, things we have passed / Perhaps a hundred times nor cared to see."[7]

Then we want to know *who* did it and *why*. We marvel at the cave paintings at Lascaux, for example, because we're sure we can detect the artist's hand behind them. If it were to turn out that the image resembling a horse was an accidental water stain, we'd dismiss it as merely quaint. When we see a Kandinsky painting or hear Arnold Schoenberg's music for the first time, we may worry perhaps that a child could have done it—or an animal or even a machine. Douglas Hofstadter has said it would be "a tragedy" if a computer program could emulate the artistic genius of Wolfgang Amadeus Mozart: "If that's the case then I've been fooled by music all my life. I've been sucked in by a vast illusion. And that would be for me an absolute tragedy, because my entire life I've been moved by music."[8]

I once wrote a scientific paper where I pointed out striking similarities between paleolithic cave paintings and the drawings of Nadia, a four-year-old autistic girl with virtually no language. The paper caused considerable dismay among afficionados because of the implicit suggestion that the cave artists may not have meant to *communicate* anything at all.[9]

And then there's the matter of authenticity. We think most highly of a work that has been physically touched by whoever created it. An original painting by a grand master is not only worth more money than a perfect copy but is also more worth looking at. Why else would ten thousand people a day visit the National Gallery in London or thirty thousand the Louvre in Paris if it's not to stand in the very shoes of the artist? Bloomsbury's *Guide to Art* says "although copies may ape the original in every way, their artistic value has been questioned and they have little commercial worth."[10]

The problem isn't that we find copies unattractive. The original Lascaux cave is closed to visitors, but a nearby replica cave has accurate reproductions of the paintings. This replica, Lascaux II, attracts up to fifteen hundred visitors a day. But the reviews on the TripAdvisor website are revealing. People are almost unanimous in speaking of how wonderful the images are, but many warn that these are "only reproductions," and some feel they were misled because they believed they were going to see the real thing.

When the work is not a material object but a verbal or musical composition, different rules apply. If we were able to hold in our hands a manuscript penned by Shakespeare, for example, or a score by Chopin, we would certainly feel closer to the author than we do with a printed copy. We might like to hear Shakespeare in person speaking the words of Hamlet or Chopin playing the piano, but we generally have to make do with third-person performances. Nonetheless, we can at least be there when the actor or musician brings the work "to life." And this allows plenty of opportunity for aesthetic emotion to be communicated by the performer's interpretation. Live performances generally get to us much more strongly than any recording can.

I remember hearing Mstislav Rostropovich play Bach's unaccompanied cello suites at Holy Trinity church in Blythburgh,

East Suffolk, in 1964. At the end, he collapsed onto his cello, as if folding himself back into it. Because we were in a church, we were not allowed to show our feelings by applauding. The Queen Mother was in the audience, accompanied by Noel Coward. To our relief, she got up from her seat, walked down the aisle to the artist, and put her arms around him. We felt she was making the connection for all of us.

The most worrying threat to authenticity is *fraud*. On one side, there's the possibility of plagiarism, when someone steals an existing work of art and passes it off us as their own. On the other, there's the possibility of impersonation, when someone creates a new work and passes it off as the work of someone else.

With plagiarism, the impostor may convince us that we are connecting to him or her emotionally when in reality the emotions come from someone else. Both we and the genuine artist are being cheated. Neal Bowers is an American poet who discovered that several of his poems had been republished under another person's name. The plagiarism did not affect the quality of the poetry as poetry. But for Bowers, it felt like a kind of artistic unmanning: "When a poem is stolen, the creative process itself is mocked, and the victim must defend not only his individual poem but also the very ground from which that poem arises."[11]

With impersonation, the impostor may convince us we are communing with a celebrated artist whose biography we already know, when in reality the emotion is a lie. The notorious fraudster Han van Meegeren produced at least six fake paintings by Johannes Vermeer. They had nothing of the artistic quality of true Vermeers. Nonetheless, for people who believed in them, they were full of significant form. In 1937, Abraham Bredius, an art historian who had dedicated a great part of his life to the study of Vermeer, was tricked into thinking that a newly discovered painting showing Christ having supper with disciples at Emmaus might be by the artist. Shortly after having viewed the painting, he wrote an effusive article in the *Burlington Magazine*, the "art bible" of the times:

> It is a wonderful moment in the life of a lover of art when he finds himself suddenly confronted with a hitherto unknown painting by a great master, untouched, on the original canvas, and without any restoration—just as it left the painter's studio. And what a picture! Neither the beautiful signature . . . nor the *pointillés* on the bread which Christ is blessing, are necessary to convince us that we have here—I am inclined to say—*the* masterpiece of Johannes Vermeer of Delft . . . quite different from all his other paintings and yet every inch a Vermeer. In no other picture by the great master of Delft do we find such sentiment, such a profound understanding of the Bible story—a sentiment so nobly human expressed through the medium of highest art.[12]

Aesthetic emotion, through and through! It's not surprising that others, less qualified to judge, followed suit. In 1943, Nazi Field-Marshal Hermann Goering bought one of van Meegeren's Vermeers for a huge price.

The significance of authenticity has recently been brought into sharp relief by the success of artificial intelligence in creating "artificial works of art." AI trained on the works of human artists is now fully capable of producing music, poetry and painting that—even if it does not yet rival that of the great masters—appears to us to be the work of a fellow human being who intends to engage our emotions. Indeed, research has shown that, in the absence of additional clues, people cannot tell whether a particular work is *not* man-made.[13] But, here's the crucial finding: if people are tricked into believing that a man-made work has in fact been created by a machine, they consider it less beautiful.[14]

* * *

All this sits perfectly with Bell's contention that, with art, our sense of connection to the artist makes all the difference to how we feel about it. Yet the problem is that this leaves natural beauty out in the cold. With the dewy grass or the elm branches across the sky, who or what should we look up to and appreciate for *getting it right*? Where does rectitude or gratitude come in? To whom do we owe this pleasure?

I've already trailed my answer in chapter 6 when discussing how nature could act as a "placebo." It is that human beings everywhere have an inborn tendency to regard beauty wherever they come across it as the product of intelligent design. If not man-made, it is still *made*.

Artists themselves provide the clue. As Bell recognizes, artists occupy a peculiar in-between position. To be consistent, Bell has to explain where significant form comes from *originally*. According to his theory, when you or I contemplate a painting by Cézanne of Mont St. Victoire, we find ourselves relating to how Cézanne felt when he gazed on the mountain 150 years ago. But if, as Bell claimed, the mountain as a natural object does not possess significant form, to whom was Cézanne himself relating when he took up his brush and created the painting? Bell acknowledged the riddle:

> Are we to suppose, then, that the artist feels, or sometimes feels, for material beauty what we feel for a work of art? Can it be that sometimes for the artist material beauty is somehow significant—that is, capable of provoking aesthetic emotion? . . . Does he feel something behind it as we imagine that we feel something behind the forms of a work of art? Are we to suppose that the emotion which the artist expresses is an aesthetic emotion felt for something the significance of which commonly escapes our coarser sensibilities? All these are questions about which I had sooner speculate than dogmatise.[15]

But he goes on to answer his own questions when he speaks of the artist becoming aware of the world's "essential reality, of the God in everything, of the universal in the particular, of the all-pervading rhythm."[16] For a solution is at hand—namely, that Cézanne had the feeling that the mountain was already the work of an aboriginal artist. I think Cézanne himself comes close to confirming this when he writes about entering "a state of grace": "The part, the whole, the volumes, the values, the composition, the emotional quiver, everything is there. . . . Shut your eyes, wait, think of nothing. Now open them."[17] He never quite says that he is communing with God. But other artists have made the connection explicit. The sculptor Constantin Brancusi pronounced: "I'm giving you pure joy. Look at the sculpture until you see it. Those nearest to God have seen it. Simplicity is not an end in art, but one arrives at simplicity in spite of oneself, in approaching the real sense of things."[18] For Vincent van Gogh, "Christ was a greater artist than all other artists."[19] For James MacNeill Whistler: "Through [the artist's] brain . . . is distilled the refined essence of that thought which began with the Gods, and which they left him to carry out."[20] And Pablo Picasso goes further: "God is really another artist . . . like me. . . . I am God, I am God, I am God."[21]

Even the avowedly atheistic eighteenth-century philosopher Denis Diderot found himself thinking about God when, despite himself, he was transfixed into a state of reverie by a pastoral river scene: "Where am I at this moment? What is all this surrounding me? I don't know, I can't say. What's lacking? Nothing. What do I want? Nothing. If there is a God, his being must be like this, taking pleasure in himself."[22]

I like that phrase—God taking pleasure in himself. It provides a way of explaining how significant form could arise *ex nihilo*. If artists treat nature as if it were divinely inspired art, then we have significant form all the way down.

Great artists no doubt differ from the rest of us. They go further than most in interrogating nature about its origins and purposes. And they are unusually public-spirited in their mission to communicate. But if and when they see nature as the work of another artist, I'd say they are simply doing what we all have done since we were children. Bell has no reason to downplay "our coarser sensibilities." If ordinary people understood what Bell meant by the words "significant form," I expect most would assume without question that it can be found everywhere in nature. Of course it can. Arguably there's more significant form to be found in an entangled bank than in all the art galleries of the world combined.

I have to take this further. I think many of us, besides half-believing the natural world is the work of an artist, half-imagine that *we ourselves* have been involved in it. It's not just Picasso who says "I am God." Richard Jefferies was transparent about his own share in bringing beauty into existence:

> I wonder to myself how they can all get on without me—how they manage, bird and flower, without me. . . . Every blade of grass was mine, as though I had planted it separately. . . . All the grasses of the meadow were my pets, I loved them all. . . . Every wild free hawk that passed overhead in the air was mine. I joyed in his swift, careless flight, in the throw of his pinions, in his rush over the elms and miles of woodland; it was happiness to see his unchecked life. These were my pets, and all the grass. . . . I cannot think how they manage without me. . . . To-day through the window-pane I see a lark high up against the grey cloud, and hear his song. . . . So beautiful to watch as if he were my own, and I felt it all![23]

The seventeenth-century poet and mystic Thomas Traherne was equally forthright about his responsibility for dreaming up the world:

> By the very right of your senses you enjoy the world. Doth not the glory of the sun pay tribute to your sight? . . . The streets were

> mine, the temple was mine, the people were mine, their clothes and gold and silver were mine, as much as their sparkling eyes, fair skins and ruddy faces. The skies were mine, and so were the sun and moon and stars, and all the World was mine; and I the only spectator and enjoyer of it.[24]

We can all be gods and take pleasure in ourselves. And why shouldn't we? Traherne was scientifically correct: The glory of the sun does indeed pay tribute to our sight. Modern cognitive science puts us, ourselves, front and center. According to the theory of "active inference," the world as we experience it is a creative hypothesis generated by our own brains—an informed guess about our surroundings that is constantly being revised in the light of sensory input. The neuroscientist Anil Seth has called it a controlled hallucination.[25] But equally it could be called an astonishing work of self-generated art. No wonder we feel personally invested in it.

All this contributes to the moral dimension of our response to beauty. Given that cognitive beauty reassures us that we are at home in the world, this homecoming is given an interpersonal halo. Whether it's nature, God, Cézanne, or ourselves, we have someone to thank for it. If the artist is God, we're at home in the world he has strived to make good for us to live in. If the artist is Cézanne, we're at home in the world whose goodness he has strived to portray. If the artist is ourselves, we're at home in the world whose goodness reflects our own creative understanding. If the artist is blind nature, we're at home in a world where even blindness turns out to be far-seeing.

The bottom line is that our feeling for beauty is fundamentally *amicable*. As the philosopher G. E. Moore wrote in *Principia Ethica*:

> Personal affection and the appreciation of what is beautiful in Art or Nature, are good in themselves. . . . it is only for the sake of these things—in order that as much as possible of them may at some time

> exist—that any one can be justified in performing any public or private duty. . . . personal affections and aesthetic enjoyments include *all* the greatest, and by far *the greatest*, goods we can imagine.[26]

But I want to say that the "appreciation of what is beautiful" *is* a variety of "personal affection." That's why we feel virtuous (and not merely self-satisfied) when we engage with the beauties of nature—as if, rather than indulging a private appetite, we are helping to spread the joy.

"Look at the stars! look, look up at the skies! / O look at all the fire-folk sitting in the air!" Gerard Manley Hopkins calls us out to celebrate the rhyming heavens.[27] But in making the call, he, like van Gogh, is putting his own emotion into circulation (figure 15.1).

FIGURE 15.1
Vincent van Gogh, *Starry Night over the Rhone*, 1888. Musée d'Orsay, Paris. Wikicommons.

16 BEAUTY AND THE BRAIN

Readers in the know may be hoping that at this point I'll turn to neuroscience for corroboration of these ideas. I'm happy to go there, because the science fits remarkably well. But, for reasons I'll come to, I won't make it a long visit.

When the British scientist Semir Zeki launched his program of "neuroaesthetics" in 1999, he had high hopes that brain imaging would reveal the existence of a "beauty processing" center in the human brain. There have been hundreds of studies since the search to find this center began.

Typically, researchers put subjects in a brain scanner, where they are exposed to objects of different kinds. They then compare the subjects' brain activity when they judge an object beautiful to that when they judge it to be plain or neutral. The hope has been to find that one and the same part of the brain is involved in processing beauty of many kinds—so that a beautiful face, for example, lights up the same part of the brain as a beautiful sunset, a beautiful sculpture, or a beautiful idea. This approach to discovering specific brain modules has worked well in the case of other mental operations, such as language processing, moral reasoning, face recognition, and map reading.

The results for beauty have certainly been promising. Zeki himself soon discovered that beautiful music and beautiful visual art activated the same part of the frontal cortex called the medial orbito-frontal cortex (mOFC).[1] In a later study, with mathematicians as subjects, he found that beautiful mathematical equations did so as well.[2] A different research team extended these findings to beautiful faces and descriptions of beautiful moral actions (figure 16.1).[3]

Encouraged by this evidence, Zeki in 2011 not only claimed to have found the beauty center but made a radical suggestion about how to *define* beauty. Rather than relying on people's behavior or subjective reports to tell us whether they judge something to be beautiful, why not ask their brains directly? He took Edmund Burke's eighteenth-century definition of beauty ("Beauty is, for the greater part, some quality in bodies acting mechanically upon the human mind by the intervention of the senses") and modified it to read "Beauty is, for the

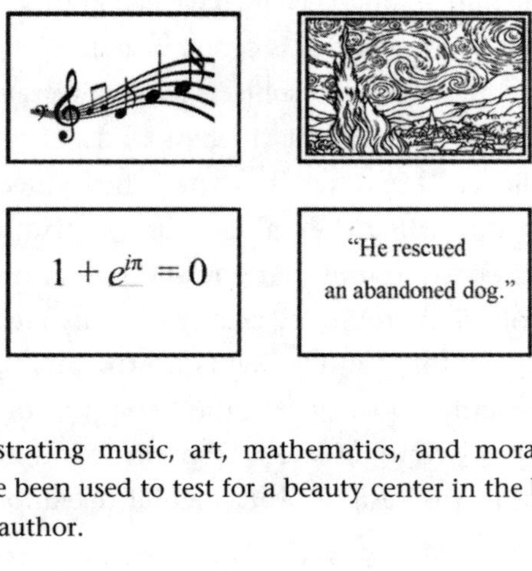

FIGURE 16.1
Images illustrating music, art, mathematics, and morality. Similar stimuli have been used to test for a beauty center in the brain. Drawings by the author.

greater part, some quality in bodies that correlates with activity in the mOFC by the intervention of the senses."[4]

It so happens that the medial orbito-frontal cortex is part of what neuroscientists have identified as the "social brain"—the network that is active when people think about their relationships and commitments to other people. A study of responses to the beauty of symmetry in abstract drawings has also implicated the social brain.[5] It all fits nicely with my own suggestion that there is indeed a social dimension to aesthetic emotion. It may seem almost too good to be true.

Unfortunately, in 2020, the authors of a wide-ranging review titled "Seeking the 'Beauty Center' in the Brain: A Meta-Analysis of fMRI Studies of Beautiful Human Faces and Visual Art" poured cold water on Zeki's central claim. In an analysis of forty-nine separate studies, they found that while the center for visual art may indeed lie where Zeki found it, the center for facial beauty lies in a separate area of frontal cortex. The authors concluded, "Our meta-analytic results revealed distinct neural specificities for visual art and face beauty but lacked evidence for the common neural basis of visual beauty. This null result suggests that the available data did not support the notion of the existence of a common brain for processing different forms of beauty."[6]

Critics of Zeki have been quick to hail this paper as a disproof of his ideas. But the sweeping negative conclusion is hardly justified by the evidence put forward. True, the analysis found that subjects in these experiments tended to employ their brains in different ways when judging art and faces, but we don't have to look far for an explanation of why this may have been so. The authors assumed that what was at issue in all forty-nine studies was "beauty." However, the details they give of the experimental protocols reveal that subjects may have been making very different kinds of judgment in the two cases. In the studies of visual art, the subjects were indeed asked to rate whether a painting was "beautiful," but in most of the studies of faces, they were asked to rate whether a face was "attractive" or "desirable" (in many cases explicitly as a sexual partner). It's rather as if people had been asked to rate the monetary value of visual art.

As we saw in the discussion of personal beauty earlier in this book, visual rhyme can indeed contribute to the attraction of a face in a potential mate. But when a person's primary motivation in gazing on a face is sexual rather than aesthetic, the emotion aroused is likely to be supplemented, if not replaced, by another species of desire, just as it will be when an art dealer gazing at a painting sees dollar signs around it.

Clive Bell, as it happens, was at pains to distance beauty from sexual attractiveness:

> With the man-in-the-street "beautiful" is more often than not synonymous with "desirable"; the word does not necessarily connote any æsthetic reaction whatever, and I am tempted to believe that in the minds of many the sexual flavour of the word is stronger than the æsthetic. . . . A beautiful picture is a photograph of a pretty girl; beautiful music, the music that provokes emotions similar to those provoked by young ladies in musical farces; and beautiful poetry, the poetry that recalls the same emotions felt, twenty years earlier, for the rector's daughter.[7]

On the whole, I'd say Zeki's claim to have found his beauty center remains alive and well. Since the findings appear to chime so well with my own ideas, you might think I'd rush to embrace them. Why look this gift horse in the mouth?

I confess my prejudice. I have long been skeptical about the value of brain imaging as a tool for psychological research, and I have particular reservations about its use in neuroaesthetics.

I can't but question the confidence of Zeki and other experimenters that subjects, lying in a brain scanner looking at a screen or listening through headphones, are processing beauty and experiencing aesthetic emotion as they might in real life. It's not just that the conditions are far from ideal. It's that, if what's key to aesthetic emotion is the feeling that somebody or something has got it right, the experimental conditions pretty much preclude any such feeling of gratitude. Zeki has never paid much attention to the interpersonal human dimension. If he has a theory of beauty, it is that it all lies in how easy it is for the brain to make sense of the stimulus at a perceptual level.

Besides the cold laboratory setting, there's another kind of barrier between the subject and the thing of beauty in these experiments. If subjects interrogate the source of their experience (What am I doing here? Why are you showing me this?), their questions are likely to be directed not to the artist but to the experimenter.

This is a well-known problem in psychological research. When an experimenter puts subjects on the spot and makes them self-conscious about their thoughts and feelings, the "demand characteristics" of the experiment get in the way. The problem is particularly acute when subjects feel that their own judgments are being judged, because they want to do well and to appear to be intelligent and cultured. I regret to say that this feature of the experiments could in itself be responsible for engaging the social brain, making it impossible to conclude anything about the social dimension of the aesthetic emotion in more natural settings.

Among all these studies, there has been no systematic study of rhyme as such—either verbal rhyme or rhyme in other sensory domains. You might have thought this would be an obvious topic for research. With verbal rhyme, at least, there's general agreement about what rhymes with what and when the rhyme is pleasing to listen to. Everyone would say that the sound of the word *cat* rhymes nicely with the sound of the word *mat* and that neither rhymes with the word *rug*. We would not be studying an emotion with all sorts of other overlays. No one would be likely to think their intelligence or good taste was being judged.

What does the brain say about rhyme? Is the response similar across domains? Do we feel some kind of gratitude when it occurs? As yet, we don't know.

Yet, the truth is, we *do* know. We know because our brains speak directly to each of us individually in the language of conscious experience—a language more clear-cut and meaningful than any computer-averaged brain scan.

The professor in Hopkins's dialogue with his student didn't need neuroscience to arrive at the insight "All beauty may be called rhyme," nor did the student need it to reply, "Yes, it is so!" Köhler didn't need neuroscience to come up with his notion of requiredness as a universal principle of perceptual organization. Bell didn't need it to recognize how the psychic presence of an artist makes all the dfference to people's emotional response.

You may or may not have been inclined to say "Yes, it is so" about the arguments presented in this book. But to get there, I'm sure you will not have had to by-pass your mind and ask your brain.

17 RHYME'S REASONS

FIGURE 17.1
Gwen Raverat, *Poplars in France*, 1916, woodcut.

When the biologist J. B. S. Haldane was asked by a group of theologians what his studies of the natural world had led him to conclude about God, he replied, "He has an inordinate fondness for beetles." The arguments with which I opened this book pay God an even greater compliment: He has an inordinate fondness for rhyming beauty (figure 17.1).

I said at the start that science—without God—is short of answers as to why this is so. But I don't think this need be the case any longer. In the preceding pages, we've discussed how rhyme affects us cognitively and emotionally and how being attracted to it benefits us. We've seen how rhyme can trigger in us the feeling that the architect of the world has "got it right."

To explain why the world is so beautiful, it remains to explain why, as a matter of fact, there is so much rhyme to be found in the world. I'm going to bring it down to four factors:

- Rhyme is in the world's DNA.
- Rhyming things endure.
- The more we look for rhyme, the more we find.
- As the world evolves, the more things there are to rhyme.

* * *

RHYME IS IN THE WORLD'S DNA

In his book *A Beautiful Question: Finding Nature's Deep Design*, the Nobel Prize–winning physicist Frank Wilczek makes a surprising claim:

> Human appreciation of the fundamental laws of Nature is a recent development on evolutionary or even historical time scales. Moreover, those laws reveal themselves only after elaborate operations—looking through sophisticated microscopes and telescopes, tearing atoms and nuclei apart, and processing long chains of mathematical reasoning—that do not come naturally. Our sense of beauty is not in any direct way adapted to Nature's fundamental workings.[1]

I think Wilczek is quite wrong. The fact is nature wears her fundamental workings on her shirtsleeves. They are revealed over and again in the spectacular phenomena we regularly encounter at the surface of reality. True, nature's *laws* may lie hidden. Looking at a whirlpool, we don't see the Coriolis forces that determine its direction of spin. Looking at the seedhead of a sunflower, we don't see a Fibonacci series. I won't say (though I'd like to) that what we see is phenomena taking pleasure in existing. But I would say that what we see is a pool or a plant in tune with itself.

In the case of the living things—cats, apples, daisies, other humans—that supply so much of the rhyme in our environment, it is literally in their DNA.

First, the information coded in the genes supervises the building of an individual body. Starting with just one fertilized egg, there's a cascade of cell division that branches to give rise to specialized tissues and repeated segments. The body ends up having anatomical parts that rhyme—finger with finger, tooth with tooth, breast with breast, leaf with leaf, berry with berry. Meanwhile, organs and functional systems emerge that rhyme reciprocally, providing mutual support at a functional level.

Second, the body buds off special reproductive cells containing copies of the DNA that go on to seed distinct new individuals. These individuals rhyme one whole body with another. Within a family, a child closely resembles its siblings and parents, not so much its grandparents, less still its cousins, and so on. Over the course of generations, lines of descent drift apart, leading to new species that rhyme with related species but in lesser ways.

When it comes to nonliving things, growth and reduplication also occur but not under such tight control. Clouds enlarge and bud off cloudlets, waves give rise to wavelets, crystals seed more crystals, and so on. Here there is no DNA to ensure that offspring resemble their parents. Nevertheless, the laws of nature see to it that there are "attractor states." Once established, these ways of existing resist change because of their internal dynamics, and nearby states tend to drift toward them and be captured by them. Examples are a whirlpool that reconstitutes itself after being broken up, a round soap bubble that returns to its shape if it's distorted, a swinging pendulum that resumes its periodic motion if it's interrupted, a gyroscope that rights itself.

Attractor states don't actively replicate themselves as life does, but they are likely to "pop up spontaneously" when conditions are favorable. So eddies form in the vicinity of a whirlpool, and freezing moist air precipitates new crystals of snow.

Attractors often have internal rhymes. And it's easy to see intuitively why this should be so. When something is made up of parts that are in balance, or reciprocate, these parts are able to borrow strength from each other, giving the whole a robustness it would not otherwise possess.

RHYMING THINGS ENDURE

For all these reasons, things that possess internal rhymes have a propensity to increase in number. But they also have individual staying power and so tend to outlast things that don't.

Again, life is the paradigm example. The internal rhymes of a living body are designed to promote overall health. They provide checks and balances that continually correct for deviations from the goal state. It's this that enables the individual organism to endure over long time periods. Life itself is a kind of attractor state.

When the correction mechanism fails internally or is overwhelmed from outside, the organism falls sick, often resulting

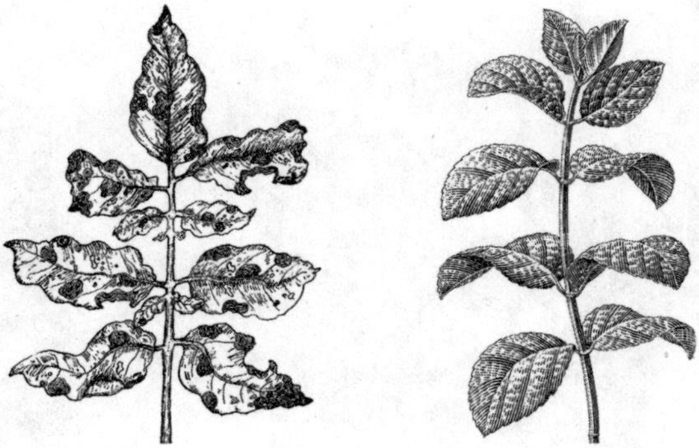

FIGURE 17.2
Diseased and healthy plants. Drawings by the author.

in a manifest lack of balance. You have only to see a tree with canker or a duck with bird flu to know how *ugly* sickness is. Compare the two plant leaves in figure 17.2.

The fact that rhyme is a good indicator of health can be exploited by organisms that want to *pretend* to be unhealthy in order to mislead a predator. When a sensitive mimosa is touched, it droops its leaves to appear to be sick and not worth eating. Using the opposite strategy, when a plover near its nest is approached by a predator, it moves away from the nest and adopts a broken-wing display to appear to be an easy catch.

As we saw earlier, rhyme is an indicator of health and staying power in nonliving systems too. Thus, for example, a rhyming physical structure is more likely to withstand environmental challenges. Compare the prospects in a gale of the two versions of the Eddystone lighthouse in Cornwall shown in figure 17.3. Henry Winstanley's wooden structure, built 1698, lasted five years; John Smeaton's, built 1759, more than a century.

FIGURE 17.3
Two designs for the Eddystone lighthouse—by Henry Winstanley (left) and John Smeaton (right). From John Smeaton, *A Narrative of the Building and a Description of the Construction of the Edystone Lighthouse with Stone* (Printed for the author by H. Hughs, sold by G. Nicol, 1791), plates 5 and 13. Public domain.

But it isn't only material structures that are likely to survive because they rhyme. It's the same for conceptual structures too: Ideas can be mutually supportive. It's true that conceptual rhymes sometimes turn out to be spurious. As we saw in chapter 4, we are sometimes seduced by accidental coincidences into believing that completely unrelated things are magically connected—woes and foes, walnuts and brains, jumps and pyramids. The "Keats heuristic"—beauty reveals truth—is certainly not entirely reliable as a guide to reality; however, it's often a valid pointer.

This isn't just because across the material world things that rhyme do typically belong together as things of a kind. It's because in the sphere of logic and science, certain ideas that rhyme *necessarily* belong together as conceptual truths.

Consider equations of identity—that is, equations that express the truth that one thing *is equal to* another: "Paris is the capital of France," "Water is H_2O," "$E = MC^2$." Because the two sides of any such equation represent *the same thing under a different description,* rhyme is a prerequisite for an identity equation to be true. Equations where the two sides don't rhyme must be false.

Compare "Paris is the capital of France" to "London is the capital of France," or "$E = MC^2$" to "$E = MC^3$." The falsehood, like a sick leaf or an unbalanced lighthouse, is ugly and lacks staying power.

The result is that, as the world of ideas evolves, truths generally see off the competition. Even if a truth is lost or becomes distorted, the chances are that it will reemerge. Thus, truths, like other forms of rhyme, accumulate around us. Even if it does not always seem so, every generation of humans is exposed to more—beautiful—truths than the one before.

THE MORE WE LOOK FOR RHYME, THE MORE WE FIND

The French sage Henri Poincaré wrote:

> The savant does not study nature because it is useful; he studies it because he takes delight in it, and he takes delight in it because it is beautiful. If nature were not beautiful, it would not be worth knowing, and life would not be worth living. . . . I speak of that profounder beauty which comes from the harmonious order of the parts, and which a pure intelligence can grasp.[2]

For humans, there are few if any brakes on this pure grasping intelligence. We find almost everything that's beautiful in nature worth knowing. We may not want to have sex with everything, we may not want to eat everything, we may not want to live everywhere, but we do want to understand everything.

In practice, there will be limits to how far this goes. There will be cognitive limits to *what we can know*, because we simply aren't mentally equipped to get our minds round certain forms of understanding. There will be practical limits to *what we have the time and opportunity to know*, because there will always be other things we have to do. And there will be factual limits to *what there is to know*, because in some environments, we may actually run out of cognitive challenges.

However, there's no reason to think these limits are fixed for all people for all time. In chapter 10, I described my experiment on how monkeys acquire a new way of seeing, where I showed how having the chance to watch another monkey's private behavior leads a monkey to look at new examples of private behavior with a new degree of discernment. It's a small example. But it shows how the comprehensibility of the world is in the eye of the beholder. As *we* grow more sophisticated, new worlds open.

The human capacity for understanding has been expanding for several reasons. One is the genetic evolution of the human brain. As our brains have evolved in size and layout, our capacity for processing information and seeing patterns in the data has been steadily increasing (and is now far beyond the capacity of a chimpanzee). The other important reason is the cultural evolution of the human mind.

With the development of language and the externalization of intelligence and knowledge, the tools of thought at our disposal have grown ever sharper and more ingenious. We can now make sense of things that our ancestors born fifty thousand years ago, who had the same innate intelligence as we have, could not have begun to. Indeed, the comparison might be much more recent. Consider the fact that a high school student today understands the world far better than Plato did just 2,500 years ago—not because she has a better brain than Plato (she probably has a lower IQ) but because she has better ideas and theories to work with.

Remarkably, Thomas Reid saw all this:

> We have reason to believe, not only that the beauties we see in nature are real, and not fanciful, but that there are thousands which our faculties are [as yet] too dull to perceive. . . . The man who is skilled in painting or statuary sees more of the beauty of a fine picture or statue than a common spectator. The same thing holds in all the fine arts. The most perfect works of art have a beauty that strikes even the rude and ignorant; but they see only a small part of that beauty which is seen in such works by those who understand them perfectly, and can produce them. This may be applied with no less justice to the works of nature. They have a beauty that strikes even the ignorant and inattentive. But the more we discover of their structure, of their mutual relations, and of the laws by which they are governed, the greater beauty, and the more delightful marks of art, wisdom, and goodness, we discern.[3]

Reid did not expect discovery could go all the way. He professed to believe that only God himself could get the full picture: "Superior beings may see more than we; but He only who made them, and upon a review pronounced them all to be 'very good,' can see all their beauty."[4]

Setting aside Reid's reverential hiccup at the end, I'd say that burgeoning human intelligence is as good an answer as any as to why the beauty of the world is so abundant and growing all the time.

I want to bring out one more answer—an explanation that Reid himself, who believed that God made the world in a single spasm of creation, could never have appreciated. It's that, as the universe has slowly evolved from formless matter, there has been a steady increase in what there is to know that continues to this day. It's not just that we humans get better at comprehending what's out there. It's that what's out there offers us more to comprehend.

AS THE WORLD EVOLVES, THE MORE THINGS THERE ARE TO RHYME

As Robert Louis Stevenson wrote in *A Child's Garden of Verses*, "The world is so full of a number of things, I think we should all be as happy as kings."[5] Yes, we should. And indeed, we are. If we have one reason above all to be happy with the world we live in, it is that the world is a mosaic of things characterized by intrinsic properties that make them what they are. Thing-hood is a constant source of cognitive delight because it reveals how the world is structured deep down. And our getting to recognize the surface patterns is the first and crucial step in making sense of what lies beneath.

* * *

Yet there remains an open question: How come the world—our world—is made like this? What if it wasn't? What if there weren't any "things"? It's not a question most people would think to ask. But the answer is worth pondering.

When the universe was formed, at the time of the Big Bang fifteen billion years ago, there weren't things of any kind at all, only a formless field of energy. From then on, however, the story was of one of ever-increasing differentiation. First came the fundamental particles. These came together to form atoms, the atoms combined to form molecules, the molecules to form materials, and the materials to form objects. At every stage, things new to the universe were coming into being. Stars, planets, moons. Volcanoes, mountains, clouds, caves, rivers, seas. Winds, rainstorms, thunder, lightning.

But then, about four billion years ago on earth (and possibly only on earth), life began to evolve. And, with it, thing-hood took off as never before. Living cells were formed, cells combined to form organisms, plant and animal species evolved, organisms developed body parts. The new world contained jellyfish, elephants, noses, flowers, skeletons, headaches, nests, pimples, and pine cones.

Finally, a few hundred thousand years ago, human beings weighed in and began to add countless kinds of manufactured objects to the inventory. Knives, hats, wheels, chimneys, bottles, string. Then, with the advent of language, they invented thing-like concepts—numbers, months, morals.

Today we give names to many of these things. The English language has about eighty thousand "common nouns"—words that name a kind of entity that exists in several forms (as distinct from "proper nouns" that name one thing in particular). Every common noun picks out a set of things that are alike but different. For every set, there are neighboring sets that are different but alike. And so on, up and down the taxonomic tree.

It's thanks to all this that we now live in a world of quite astonishing diversity—well-ordered, comprehensible diversity. Ludwig Wittgenstein opens his major philosophical work, the *Tractatus Logico-Philosophicus*, with the oddly empty statement "Die Welt ist alles, was der Fall ist," often translated as "The world is everything that is the case." A much more revealing and scientifically interesting statement would be "The world is every *kind of thing* that *has become* the case."

Is thing-making—the propensity for giving rise to kinds of thing that form a nested hierarchy—a "law of nature"? Perhaps it's more of a habit than a law—a pattern that has emerged as things work out in practice.[6] But it's a habit that has ensured that the world—at least the world we humans inhabit—has eventually become pervaded by rhyme. Contrary to Wilczek, our sense of beauty is indeed directly and primarily adapted to this, most fundamental, feature of nature's workings.

How lucky we are here on earth! Things could have worked out very differently. Tweak the initial conditions at the Big Bang, and the universe might have remained a formless slurry. Remove the evolution of life, and there would be no rhyming plants and animals. Remove humans, and there would be few rhyming artefacts, fewer rhyming ideas, and no rhyming words.

When humans travel—as they soon will—to lifeless Mars, they should be prepared for aesthetic disappointment. While we've found eighty thousand kinds of thing to name on earth—all potential rhymers—Mars will lack almost all of them and will have few if any Martian ones to show of its own. It won't be every day that Mars arranges itself into a poem.

* * *

"The time has come," the Walrus said,
"To talk of many things:
Of shoes—and ships—and sealing-wax—
Of cabbages—and kings—."[7]

Why is our world so beautiful? It's because, thanks to the local and exceptional creative forces here on earth, there are so many things for us to talk about and understand. We see how good it all is, and—hardly believing our luck—we embrace the creator, little realizing how much of the art is our own.

Consider stars repeated in a lake;
mountains which, twinned by their reflections, make
beauty twofold; willows and reeds that gaze
upon their doubles down the waterways.

See how no sod, however single-hearted,
can from his constant shadow-self be parted,
no wave from wave until along the beach
identities are shattered. Each to each,
shadow to substance, echo to the song,
paired limbs, paired leaves, like lovers all belong.

So richly has this symmetry of rhyme
enhanced our world through immemorial time,
men's very words most move us when they chime.
—Frances Higginson Savage, *The Symmetry of Rhyme*[8]

NOTES

CHAPTER 1

1. Jemima Harrison, dir., *The Family That Walks on All Fours*, Passionate Productions, aired on BBC Two, March 17, 2006.

2. Samuel Taylor Coleridge, *Anima Poetae*, ed. Ernest Hartley Coleridge (William Heinemann, 1895), chapter VIII, https://www.gutenberg.org/ebooks/41705.epub.images.

3. Jorge Luis Borges, "The Wall and the Books," in *Labyrinths: Selected Stories and Other Writings*, principal ed. and trans. James Irby (New Directions, 1962), 188.

4. Cecil Alexander, "All Things Bright and Beautiful," in *Hymns for Little Children* (Herman Hooker, 1848), 27.

5. See the overview by Peter Williams in "Aesthetic Arguments for the Existence of God," *Quodlibet Journal* 3, no. 3 (Summer 2001).

6. Immanuel Kant, *Critique of Judgment* (1790), trans. Nicholas Walker (Oxford University Press, 2009), book I.i.2.

7. Theophile Gautier, *Mademoiselle de Maupin* (1835), trans. I. G. Burnham (George Barrie and Sons, 1887), 31: "Nothing that is beautiful is indispensable to life. You might suppress flowers, and the world would not suffer materially; yet who would wish that there were no

more flowers? I would rather give up potatoes than roses, and I think that there is none but an utilitarian in the world capable of pulling up a bed of tulips in order to plant cabbages therein. What is the use of women's beauty? Provided that a woman be medically well formed, and in condition to bear children, she will always be good enough for economists. What is the good of music? Of painting? Who would be foolish enough to prefer Mozart to Monsieur Carrel, and Michael Angelo to the inventor of white mustard? There is nothing truly beautiful but that which can never be of any use whatsoever; everything useful is ugly, for it is the expression of some need, and man's needs are ignoble and disgusting like his own poor and infirm nature. The most useful place in a house is the water-closet."

8. Thomas Reid, "Of Beauty" (chapter 4 of essay VIII, "Of Taste"), in *Essays on the Intellectual Powers of Man* (1785) (MIT Press, 1969), 779.

9. Reid, 785.

10. Reid, 785.

11. Reid, 780.

12. Johann Herbart, *Practical Philosophy* (1808), quoted in *Philosophies of Beauty: From Socrates to Robert Bridges, Being the Sources of Aesthetic Theory*, ed. E. F. Carritt (Oxford University Press, 1931), 153.

13. Gerard Manley Hopkins, "On the Origins of Beauty: A Platonic Dialogue" (1865), in *The Journals and Papers of Gerard Manley Hopkins*, ed. Humphry House and Graham Storey (Oxford University Press, 1959), 86–114.

14. Ernst Gombrich, *The Story of Art* (New York: Phaidon, 1951), 22.

15. Maureen Duffy, "Review of *In the Shadow of Man*," *New Statesman* (January 1971).

CHAPTER 2

1. Gerard Manley Hopkins, *On the Origins of Beauty: A Platonic Dialogue* (1865), in *The Journals and Papers of Gerard Manley Hopkins*, ed. Humphry House and Graham Storey (Oxford University Press, 1959), 86–114.

2. Clive Bell, *Art* (Chatto and Windus, 1915), 6.

CHAPTER 4

1. Louis J. Halle, "The Flight of Seabirds," *Virginia Quarterly Review* 55, no. 1 (1979): 22–40.

2. Gerard Manley Hopkins, "It Was a Hard Thing to Undo This Knot" (1864), in *Poems of Gerard Manley Hopkins*, ed. Robert Bridges (Oxford University Press, 1948), 128.

3. Ian Christopher McManus and P. Weatherby, "The Golden Section and the Aesthetics of Form and Composition: A Cognitive Model," *Empirical Studies of the Arts* 15 (1997): 210.

4. Plato, *Phaedo* (399 BC), in *The Dialogues of Plato*, trans. Benjamin Jowett, vol. 2 (Oxford University Press, 1892), 4.

5. It even works quite well in French "translation" in Frank L. Warrin, "Le Jaseroque," *The New Yorker*, January 10, 1931, 52:

> Il brilgue: les tôves lubricilleux
> Se gyrent en vrillant dans le guave.
> Enmîmés sont les gougebosqueux
> Et le môme rade horsgrave.

6. Zora Neale Hurston, *Their Eyes Were Watching God* (1937) (Virago, 2020), 191.

7. Mathew Arnold, "Dover Beach" (1851), in *New Poems* (Macmillan, 1867).

8. Alice Major, "Word Shapes and Rhymescapes: Translating Translation Symmetry into Music and Poetry," *Math Horizons* (February 2013): 22.

9. Émile Zola, *Salon 1868* (1868), quoted in *The Great Masters* (Quantum Books, 2003), 279–319.

10. Wallace Stevens, from "Adagia," *Poetry* 90 (1957): 40–44.

11. Robert Browning, "Fra Lippo Lippi," in *Men and Women* (Chapman and Hall, 1855).

12. The story is explored in Iliana Gutierrez, "Pablo Picasso: The Many Iterations of *Las Meninas*," *Noble Oceans* (blog), March 29, 2017, https://www.nobleoceans.com/artists/2017/4/4/pablo-picasso-the-many-iterations-of-las-meninas.

13. Pablo Picasso, remark to Françoise Gilot, quoted in Françoise Gilot and Carlton Lake, *Life with Picasso* (McGraw Hill, 1964), 120.

14. Friedrich Nietzsche, *The Gay Science* (1887), trans. Walter Kauffman (Vintage Books, 1974), 139–140.

15. Matthew McGlone and Jessica Tofighbakhsh, "The Keats Heuristic: Rhyme as Reason in Aphorism Interpretation," *Poetics* 26 (1999): 235–244.

16. Vincenzo Orofino, "A Quantitative Astronomical Analysis of the Orion Correlation Theory," ArXiv, Cornell University, 2014, https://doi.org/10.48550/arXiv.1109.6266.

17. Dennett's "haptic whittles" were exhibited at a one-man show in New York in 2017. Daniel Dennett, *Haptic Whittles*, February 11–March 26, 2017, Underdonk, New York, https://www.underdonk.com/exhibitions/haptic-whittles/.

18. Oliver Sacks, "Mendeleev's Garden," in *Uncle Tungsten: Memories of a Chemical Boyhood* (Picador, 2001), 181.

19. Freeman Dyson, quoted in Sacks, "Mendeleev's Garden."

20. Primo Levi, *The Periodic Table*, trans. Raymond Rosenthal (Schocken Books, 1984), 43.

21. Francis Crick, letter from Francis Crick to Michael Crick, March 15, 1953, Wellcome Collection, London, PP/CRI/D/4/3, https://wellcomecollection.org/works/v3ndr2ux/items.

CHAPTER 5

1. Mark Collard and Francesco d'Errico, chairs, Symposium on Body Modification: Anatomy, Alteration, and Art in Anthropogeny, Center for Academic Research and Training in Anthropogeny, University of California, San Diego, February 9, 2024, https://carta.anthropogeny.org/events/body-modification-anatomy-alteration-and-art-anthropogeny.

2. Jonathan Jones, "And the Winner Is . . . How a Bitter Painting Contest Between Michelangelo and Leonardo Became One of the

Most Extraordinary Episodes of the Renaissance," *The Guardian*, October 22, 2002, https://www.theguardian.com/culture/2002/oct/22/artsfeatures.highereducation.

3. It worked. A. V. Hill went on to win the Nobel Prize for medicine in 1923. His wife, Margaret Keynes, became a pioneer of social welfare.

4. Edward Wilson, *Biophilia: The Human Bond with Other Species* (Harvard University Press, 1984).

5. Richard Taylor, "Fractals in Psychology and Art" (blog), University of Oregon, February 3, 2016, https://blogs.uoregon.edu/richardtaylor/2016/02/03/human-physiological-responses-to-fractals-in-nature-and-art/; Florence Williams, "Feel-Good Fractals: From Ocean Waves to Jackson Pollock's Art," from *The Nature Fix: Why Nature Makes Us Happier, Healthier, and More Creative* (W. W. Norton, 2017), *Aeon*, January 26, 2017, https://aeon.co/ideas/feel-good-fractals-from-ocean-waves-to-jackson-pollocks-art.

6. See, for example, Ulrika Stigsdotter: "People think that you have to walk in green fields to benefit your health, but actually there's lots of evidence that walking round cities is good for you too." Cited in Helen Thomson, "Take a Hike," *New Scientist* 266, no. 3541 (May 3, 2025): 38–41.

7. Andrew Curry, "Gobekli Tepe: The World's First Temple?," *Smithsonian*, November 2008.

8. Ernst Gombrich, "The Miracle at Chauvet," *New York Review of Books*, November 14, 1996, 8.

CHAPTER 6

1. John dos Passos, *The Big Money* (1936), book 3 of the *U.S.A.* trilogy (Penguin, 1969), 1080.

2. Jos F. Brosschot, Bart Verkuil, and Julian F. Thayer, "Generalized Unsafety Theory of Stress: Unsafe Environments and Conditions, and the Default Stress Response," *International Journal of Environmental Research and Public Health* 15 (2018): 464.

3. Nicholas Humphrey and John Skoyles, "The Evolutionary Psychology of Healing: A Human Success Story," *Current Biology* 22 (2012): R1–R4.

4. R. S. Ulrich, "View Through a Window May Influence Recovery from Surgery," *Science* 224, no. 4647 (April 27, 1984): 420–421, DOI: 10.1126/science.6143402, PMID: 6143402.

5. Kathleen D. Vohs, Joseph P. Redden, and Ryan Rahinel, "Physical Order Produces Healthy Choices, Generosity, and Conventionality, Whereas Disorder Produces Creativity," *Psychological Science* 24, no. 9 (2013): 1860–1867, DOI: 10.1177/0956797613480186.

6. David Sloan-Wilson, *The Neighborhood Project: Using Evolution to Improve My City, One Block at a Time* (Little, Brown, 2011).

7. Haruaki Fukuda, Hiroaki Suzuki, and Ayum Yamada, "Implicit Influence of Other's Intention in Prisoner's Dilemma Game," presented at the 15th Annual Meeting of the Association for the Scientific Study of Consciousness, June 9–12, 2011, Kyoto, Japan, Primate Research Institute, Kyoto University.

8. S. D. Bilbo, D. L. Brazen, N. Quran, L. He, and R. J. Nelson, "Short Day Lengths Attenuate the Symptoms of Infection in Siberian Hamsters." *Proceedings of the Royal Society of London, Series B: Biological Sciences* 269 (2002): 447–454.

9. Layamon, *Brut* (*The Chronicle of Britain*) (1215), quoted in Dan Jones, "New Light on Stonehenge," *Smithsonian*, October 2008, 46.

10. George Borrow, *Lavengro: The Scholar, the Gypsy, the Priest* (1851) (John Murray, 1900), 180.

11. Clive Bell, *Art* (Chatto and Windus, 1924), 50.

12. Jonathan Jong, "Are Children Creationists?," in *Experimenting with Religion: The New Science of Belief* (Oxford Academic, 2023), 40–45.

13. Gen. 9:16, King James Version.

CHAPTER 7

1. Charles Darwin, *On the Origin of Species by Means of Natural Selection, or the Preservation of Favoured Races in the Struggle for Life* (John Murray, 1859), 490.

CHAPTER 8

1. Sara Nasiri, Julien Helsper, Matthias Jung, and Madjid Fathi, "DePicT Melanoma Deep-CLASS: A Deep Convolutional Neural Networks Approach to Classify Skin Lesion Images," *BMC Bioinformatics* 21 (suppl. 2), no. 84 (March 11, 2020): fig. 7.

CHAPTER 9

1. W. H. Auden, *The Dyer's Hand and Other Essays* (Faber and Faber, 1948), 19.

2. Stanislas Ulam, *Adventures of a Mathematician* (Scribner's, 1976), 180–181.

3. John Hollander, *Rhyme's Reason: A Guide to English Verse* (Yale University Press, 2001). 52.

4. Matt Ridley, "When Ideas Have Sex," TED Talk discussed in *The Rational Optimist: How Prosperity Evolves* (Harper Collins, 2010).

5. The aphorism "How do I know what I think until I see what I say?" is often attributed to E. M. Forster but appears to have been coined by Graham Wallas in *The Art of Thought* (Harcourt, Brace, 1926), 106: "The little girl had the making of a poet in her who, being told to be sure of her meaning before she spoke, said, 'How can I know what I think till I see what I say?'"

6. Yoon Mi Oh, "Linguistic Complexity and Information: Quantitative Approaches," PhD thesis, University of Lyon, 2015.

7. *Colloque d'esthétique appliquée à la création du paysage urban: Arc-et-Senans, 24–26 Septembre 1973* (Copédith, 1975).

8. Joseph Brodsky, "On 'September 1, 1939' by W. H. Auden," in *Less Than One: Selected Essays* (Viking Penguin, 1987), 350.

9. Percy Bysshe Shelley, "A Defence of Poetry" (1821), in *Selected Prose Works of Shelley* (Watts. 1915), 75.

CHAPTER 10

1. Aristotle, *Poetics*, IV, trans. Ingram Bywater (Clarendon Press, 1920), 29.

2. Nicholas Humphrey, "Interest and Pleasure: Two Determinants of a Monkey's Visual Preferences," *Perception* 1 (1972): 395–416.

3. Nicholas Humphrey and Graham Keeble, "The Reactions of Monkeys to 'Fearsome' Pictures," *Nature* 251 (1974): 500–502.

4. I first floated this idea in an essay. Nicholas Humphrey, "The Illusion of Beauty," *Perception* 2 (1973): 429–439.

5. Nicholas Humphrey, "Species and Individuals in the Perceptual World of Monkeys," *Perception* 3 (1974): 105–114.

6. Nicholas Humphrey and Graham Keeble, "How Monkeys Acquire a New Way of Seeing," *Perception* 5 (1976): 51–56.

7. Patrick Jackson and Patrick Bateson, "Imprinting and Exploration of Slight Novelty in Chicks," *Nature* 251 (1974): 609–610.

8. Ronald Reagan (1964), quoted in Thomas H. Harris, "How Many Trees Do You Need to See? Said the Governor," *New York Times*, June 24, 1973, https://www.nytimes.com/1973/06/24/archives/how-many-trees-do-you-need-to-see-said-the-governor-opposed-new.html.

CHAPTER 11

1. Jerome Kagan, "Attention and Psychological Change in the Young Child," *Science* 170 (1970): 826–832.

2. Elizabeth Spelke, *What Babies Know: Core Knowledge and Composition* (Oxford University Press, 2022).

3. Gen. 2:19, King James Version.

4. Carolus Linnaeus, *Systema Naturae* (1735), trans. M. S. J. Engel-Ledeboer and H. Engel (B. de Graaf, 1964), 19 [facsimile of the first edition].

5. Richard Wilbur, "Poetry and Landscape," in *The New Landscape in Art and Science*, ed. G. Kepes (Paul Theobald, 1956), 86–89.

6. Robert Bridges, "The Idle Flowers," in *Poetical Works of Robert Bridges* (Smith, Elder & Co., 1898).

7. A. P. Herbert (1932), quoted in *The Gardener's Companion*, ed. Miles Hadfield (Dent, 1936), 194.

8. Richard Porter, quoted in *Sunday Times*, June 16, 1974.

9. Ivan Pavlov, "The Reflex of Purpose" (1928), in *Lectures on Conditioned Reflexes*, vol. 1 (Lawrence and Wishart, 1941), 277.

10. The description of Freud's collection, including the quotations, is taken from Russell W. Belk, Melanie Wallendorf, John F. Sherry, and Morris B. Holbrook, "Collecting in a Consumer Culture," in *Highways and Buyways: Naturalistic Research from the Consumer Behavior Odyssey*, ed. Russell Belk (Association for Consumer Research, 1991), 178–215. See also Ro Spankie, *Sigmund Freud's Desk: An Anecdoted Guide* (Freud Museum, 2015).

11. *The Guardian*, October 20, 1973 [no longer available].

12. David Lindo, "How to Be a Twitcher," *Discover Wildlife*, https://www.discoverwildlife.com/how-to/watch-wildlife/how-to-be-a-twitcher.

13. Bec Whetham, "Twitching: The Obsessive World of Extreme Birdwatching," ABC News, June 30, 2018, https://www.abc.net.au/news/2018-07-01/the-obsessive-world-of-twitching/9718740.

14. John Neville Keynes's first book was *Formal Logic: Including a Generalisation of Logical Processes in their Application to Complex Inferences* (Cambridge University Press, 1884).

CHAPTER 12

1. David Hume, *An Enquiry Concerning Human Understanding* (1748), ed. Peter Millikan (Oxford University Press, 2007), 1.10.

2. The monkeys responded in the same way to an unfocused movie as to a movie bathed in red light, which is a color monkeys find emotionally upsetting. The mathematical analysis showing that this was due to "unpleasure" and not "uninterest" is at the end of my paper on interest and pleasure. Nicolas Humphrey, "Interest and Pleasure: Two Determinants of a Monkey's Visual Preferences," *Perception* 1 (1972): 395–416.

3. Donald O. Hebb, "On the Nature of Fear," *Psychological Review* 53 (1946): 268.

4. Donald O. Hebb, *Textbook of Psychology* (W. Saunders, 1958), 163.

5. Mary Douglas, *Purity and Danger: An Analysis of Concepts of Pollution and Taboo* (Routledge and Kegan Paul, 1966), 55.

6. Gertrude Stein, "The Autobiography of Alice B. Toklas" (excerpt), *The Atlantic Monthly*, May 1933, 15.

7. Pablo Picasso, "Picasso Speaks," *The Arts* (New York), May 1923, 315–326.

8. Chris Chapman, Sue Andrew, and Tom Greeves, *The Three Hares: A Curiosity Worth Regarding* (Skerryvore Productions, 2016). Information about the three hares project and a PDF of the book can be found at https://www.chrischapmanphotography.co.uk/hares/page7.htm.

9. Colin McGinn, "Can We Solve the Mind-Body Problem?," *Mind* 98 (1989): 349–366.

10. Recent research on awe owes much to Dacher Keltner and Jonathan Haidt, "Approaching Awe, a Moral, Spiritual, and Aesthetic Emotion," *Cognition and Emotion* 17 (2003): 297–314. In the authors' words, "We propose that prototypical awe involves a challenge to or negation of mental structures when they fail to make sense of an experience of something vast. Such experiences can be disorienting and even frightening."

11. Maria Monroy and Dacher Keltner, "Awe as a Pathway to Mental and Physical Health," *Perspectives on Psychological Science* 20 (2022): 1–12; Ji Young Song, Christoph Klebl, and Brock Bastian, "Awe Promotes Moral Expansiveness via the Small-Self," *Frontiers of. Psychology* 14 (2023):1097627.

CHAPTER 13

1. Nelson Goodman, "Art and Inquiry," *Proceedings and Addresses of the American Philosophical Association* 41 (1967–1968): 5–19.

CHAPTER 14

1. Alison Gopnik, "Explanation as Orgasm," *Minds and Machines* 8 (1998): 101–118.

2. Wolfgang Köhler, *The Mentality of Apes* (1921), trans. Ella Winter (Kegan Paul, Trench, Trubner, 1925).

3. Wolfgang Köhler, *The Place of Value in a World of Facts* (Liveright, 1938).

4. Köhler, *The Place of Value in a World of Facts*, 100.

5. Clive Bell *Art* (Chatto and Windus,1915), 65.

6. Roger Scruton, *Beauty: A Very Short Introduction* (Oxford University Press, 2011), 55.

7. Novalis, *Novalis Schriften* (1837), ed. Jacob Minor, vol. 2 (Eugen Diedrichs, 1907), 179.

8. Wilfred Sellars, "Philosophy and the Scientific Image of Man," in *Frontiers of Science and Philosophy*, ed. Robert Colodny (University of Pittsburgh Press, 1962), 35.

9. Samuel Taylor Coleridge, *Anima Poetae*, ed. Ernest Hartley Coleridge (William Heinemann, 1895), chapter VIII, https://www.gutenberg.org/ebooks/41705.epub.images; Jorge Luis Borges, "The Wall and the Books," in *Labyrinths: Selected Stories and Other Writings*, principal ed. and trans. James Irby (New Directions, 1962), 188.

10. Thomas Armstrong and Brian Detweiler-Bedell, "Beauty as an Emotion: The Exhilarating Prospect of Mastering a Challenging World," *Review of General Psychology* 12 (2008): 305–329.

CHAPTER 15

1. Clive Bell, *Art* (Chatto and Windus, 1915), 6–8.

2. Bell, *Art*, 49.

3. Paul Cézanne, quoted in Joachim Gasquet, *Cézanne: A Memoir with Conversations* (1926), trans. Christopher Pemberton (Thames & Hudson, 1991), 166.

4. Bell, *Art*, 50.

5. Richard Jefferies, *The Story of My Heart* (Longmans, Green, 1883), 76.

6. Henry David Thoreau, from October 1, 1856, in *Journal*, vol. 9, August 16, 1856–August 7, 1857, in *The Writings of Henry David Thoreau*, ed. Bradford Torrey (Houghton, Mifflin, 1906), 9:97.

7. Robert Browning, "Fra Lippo Lippi," in *Men and Women* (Chapman and Hall, 1855).

8. Douglas Hofstadter, quoted in Bob Holmes, "Requiem for the Soul," *New Scientist* (August 9, 1997), 22–27.

9. Nicholas Humphrey, "Cave Art, Autism and the Evolution of the Human Mind," *Cambridge Archaeological Journal* 8 (1999): 165–191.

10. *Bloomsbury's Guide to Art*, quoted in Patrick Lyndon, "Unoriginal Art," *Prospect* (April 2003): 14.

11. Neal Bowers, *Words for the Taking: The Hunt for a Plagiarist* (Norton, 1997).

12. Jonathan Janzen, "Han van Meegeren's Fake Vermeers," *Essential Vermeer 5.0*, https://www.essentialvermeer.com/misc/van_meegeren.html.

13. Harsha Gangadharbatla, "The Role of AI Attribution Knowledge in the Evaluation of Artwork," *Empirical Studies of the Arts* 40, no. 2 (2022): 125–142; C. Di Dio et al., "Art Made by Artificial Intelligence: The Effect of Authorship on Aesthetic Judgments," *Psychology of Aesthetics, Creativity, and the Arts* 19, no. 5 (2025): 1164–1176.

14. Marcus du Sautoy gives the telling example of a musicologist whose first response on hearing an imitation of a Bach piano piece created by David Cope was to describe it as profoundly beautiful but who completely reversed his opinion after Cope explained how it had been generated using a mathematical algorithm. See Marcus Du Sautoy, *The Creativity Code: Art and Innovation in the Age of AI* (4th Estate, 2019), 201.

15. Bell, *Art*, 52.

16. Bell, 69.

17. Paul Cézanne, quoted in Gasquet, *Cézanne*, 165.

18. Constantin Brancusi, quoted in Ionel Jianou, *Brancusi* (Tudor, 1963), 68.

19. Vincent van Gogh (1888). quoted in Joel L. Swerdlow, *National Geographic*, October 1997, 130.

20. James McNeill Whistler (1885), *Mr Whistler's Ten O'Clock* (Chatto & Windus, 1888), 16.

21. Pablo Picasso to a Spanish friend in the 1930s, quoted in John Richardson, *A Life of Picasso*, vol. 3, *The Triumphant Years, 1917–1932* (Jonathan Cape, 2007), 49.

22. Denis Diderot, *Diderot on Art*, ed. and trans. J. Goodman, vol. 2 (Yale University Press, 1995), 98.

23. Richard Jefferies, *The Story of My Heart* (Longmans, Green, 1883), 2.

24. Thomas Traherne, *Centuries of Meditation* (1670) (Dent, 1908), century 1.21.

25. Anil Seth, *Being You* (Faber, 2021).

26. G. E. Moore, *Principia Ethica* (Cambridge University Press, 1903), chap. 6, sec. 113–114.

27. Gerard Manley Hopkins, "The Starlight Night," in *Gerard Manley Hopkins: Poems and Prose*, ed. W. H. Gardner (Penguin Classics, 1985)

CHAPTER 16

1. Tomohiro Ishizu and Semir Zeki, "Toward a Brain-Based Theory of Beauty," *PLOS One* 6, no. 7 (2011): e21852.

2. Semir Zeki, John Paul Romaya, Dionigi M. T. Benincasa, and Michael F. Atiyah, "The Experience of Mathematical Beauty and Its Neural Correlates," *Frontiers of Human Neuroscience* 8 (2014): 68.

3. Tomohiro Tsukiura and R. Cabeza, "Shared Brain Activity for Aesthetic and Moral Judgments: Implications for the Beauty-Is-Good Stereotype," *Social Cognitive and Affective Neuroscience* 6 (2011): 138–148.

4. Ishizu and Zeki, "Toward a Brain-Based Theory of Beauty."

5. Thomas Jacobsen, Ricarda I. Schubotz, Lea Höfel, and D. Yves v. Cramon, "Brain Correlates of Aesthetic Judgment of Beauty," *NeuroImage* 29 (2006): 276–285.

6. Hu Chuan-Peng, Yi Huang, Simon B. Eickhoff, Kaiping Peng, and Jie Sui, "Seeking the 'Beauty Center' in the Brain: A Meta-Analysis of fMRI Studies of Beautiful Human Faces and Visual Art," *Cognitive, Affective, and Behavioral Neuroscience* 20 (2020): 1211.

7. Clive Bell, *Art* (Chatto and Windus,1915), 15.

CHAPTER 17

1. Frank Wilczek, *A Beautiful Question: Finding Nature's Deep Design* (Allen Lane, 2015), 11.

2. Henri Poincaré, *Science et méthode* (Flammarion, 1908), 22 (my translation).

3. Thomas Reid, "Of Beauty" (chapter 4 of essay VIII, "Of Taste"), in *Essays on the Intellectual Powers of Man* (1785) (MIT Press, 1969), 783.

4. Reid, 785.

5. Robert Louis Stevenson, "Happy Thought," in *A Child's Garden of Verses* (Charles Scribner's Sons, 1897), 28.

6. The neuroscientist Karl Friston believes that "things" throughout nature (at least all those worthy of the name) have an inbuilt capacity to anticipate and resist externally imposed changes of state and thus to maintain their place in the hierarchy of existents. He invokes the notion of a "Markov blanket"—an abstract, statistical skin that distinguishes every thing from everything else. By providing the thing with a model of the external world, this blanket allows the thing to adjust its internal states so as to minimize disruptive surprises. See Elise Cutts, "The Free-Energy Principle: Can One Idea Explain Why Everything Exists?," *New Scientist* 28 (October 2024): 33–36.

7. Lewis Carroll, "The Walrus and the Carpenter," in *Through the Looking Glass, and What Alice Found There* (Macmillan, 1871), 75.

8. Frances Higginson Savage, "The Symmetry of Rhyme," *Educational Forum* 31, no. 1 (1966): 78, DOI: 10.1080/00131726609338015.

INDEX

Note: Page numbers in *italics* indicate figures or tables.